ASTROLOGICAL CROSSES

Exploring the Cardinal, Fixed & Mutable Modes

Praise for Astrological Crosses

"Pauline Edward's book helps us to understand why people think and communicate the way they do, which in turn helps us to improve our relationships. That's no small feat! In depth, well-written, and informative."
—Lucy MacDonald, M.Ed., author of *Learn to Be an Optimist*

"Pauline Edward has written the best book yet about the nature of Cardinal, Fixed, and Mutable. Her readable, insightful work can help both beginning and experienced astrologers gain much understanding about life's processes. Highly recommended."
—Michael Munkasey, PMAFA, NCGR-IV

"Absolutely excellent work on the cardinal, fixed and mutable qualities of the signs. Suitable for any level of astrologer this goes into the subject at a deeper level than I've seen before. Thought provoking and intelligently written."
—*The Wessex Astrologer*

"*Astrological Crosses in Relationships* now has a prominent spot on my astrological reference bookshelf. I will return to it often, in mutable dipping and skipping for immediately useful knowledge, in a fixed desire to spur greater mastery and creative approach to my astrology practice, and in a cardinal obsession with needing and wanting to be in on a very good thing."
—Susan Kelly, author of *Be Star Chic*

ALSO BY PAULINE EDWARD

Gateway to a New World

Aquarius: The Age of Revelation, Choice and Transformation

The Healing of Humanity

The Movement of Being

Choosing the Miracle

Leaving the Desert: Embracing the Simplicity of A Course in Miracles

Making Peace with God: The Journey of a Course in Miracles Student

The Power of Time: Understanding the Cycles of Your Life's Path

L'Hermès: Dictionnaire des correspondances symboliques, with Marc Bériault and Axel Harvey

ASTROLOGICAL CROSSES

Exploring the Cardinal,
Fixed & Mutable Modes

Pauline Edward

Desert Lily Publications
Montreal, Canada

© 2013 Pauline Edward

All rights reserved. No part of this work may be reproduced or used in any form or by any means, electronic, digital or mechanical, including photocopying, recording or any retrieval system, without the prior written permission of the publisher.

Revised edition, previously published as *Astrological Crosses in Relationships: Understanding Cardinal, Fixed & Mutable Energies*, 2002, Llewellyn Publications.

For
my daughters
Natalie and Caroline

You believed in me when my confidence failed,
You lit my path when I saw only darkness,
You supported me when my strength waned,
You encouraged me when I lost hope,
You listened to me when I needed to be heard,
You celebrated with me when I triumphed.

I am truly blessed!

Contents

List of Charts xi

Acknowledgments xiii

Author's Note xv

Introduction 1

1. *A Cross by Any Other Name* 13

2. *The Cardinal Cross* 25

3. *The Fixed Signs* 45

4. *The Mutable Cross* 75

5. *The Crosses in the Life Experience* 101

6. *Working with the Crosses* 121

Bibliography & Resources 145

List of Charts

1. *John* 5
2. *Dr. Martin Luther King, Jr.* 27
3. *W. Somerset Maugham* 47
4. *Oprah Winfrey* 52
5. *Marc Edmund Jones* 55
6. *Henry Ford* 62
7. *Odile* 65
8. *Betty* 69
9. *Queen Elizabeth I* 79
10. *Charlotte Brontë* 82
11. *Mother Teresa* 94
12. *Bill Gates* 108
13. *Steve Jobs* 110
14. *Suzie* 115
15. *Rina* 127
16. *Model* 131
17. *Michael* 133
18. *Carol* 139

Acknowledgments

A special thanks to the late Marc Bériault for sharing his ideas on the crosses, and to Axel Harvey for his patience and painstaking diligence in researching and verifying birth data for this book.

I will always remain grateful for the thousands of wonderful people who have been placed on my path over the course of my life. Family, friends, and clients, each in their unique way, have helped me develop a better understanding of human nature and of astrology.

A special thank you to Michael J. Miller for his help with the layout of this new edition.

Author's Note

I have given this book a personal style and, throughout, have made liberal use of anecdotes, quotations, and examples from the actual experiences of people I have met and observed over the years, as well as from books and the media. In so doing, I hope to have provided a vivid portrayal of the crosses, enabling readers to easily apply these principles in their own lives or astrological practice.

The technical material has been kept to a minimum, so that even non astrologers can benefit from learning about the crosses. It is not necessary to be knowledgeable in the complex art of reading astrology charts in order to read this book, as the cross of the Sun sign alone will reveal much about the basic character of an individual.

2013 Edition

Other than minor layout and editorial changes, this edition of *Astrological Crosses* is basically the same as the original. While some short chapters have been merged for ease of reading, the overall layout has been tightened up to reduce page count, cut printing costs, and save trees! The subject of the crosses remains as relevant and as fascinating as ever.

Introduction

Years ago, 1987 I believe it was, I had the great fortune of attending a lecture in Ottawa given by astrologer Marc Bériault. I say "great fortune" because the concepts to which I was introduced on that Saturday afternoon have since grown and developed into the material for this book, and have provided me with key elements for unlocking some of the subtler mysteries and complexities of astrological interpretation. The odd thing is that it was not the featured subject of the afternoon that so gripped my attention, not to diminish in any way the significance of the Dark Moon Lilith, but rather the sidebar Bériault engaged us in early in the lecture, a somewhat extended digression into the world of the "crosses," as he so called them, or the "quadruplicities," or "modes," as they are more commonly known.

Following a thorough and detailed explanation of the astronomical and mathematical factors involved in the calculation of Lilith's placement in our solar system, Bériault proceeded to give example delineations of Lilith by cross placement, instead of the more typical approach of sign or even element placement. He must have drawn a roomful of blank stares at the mention of the *crosses*, for he paused, assessed his audience's response, and asked if a definition of the crosses might be in order. When the group unanimously and eagerly agreed to the interruption, in true Aquarian style our lecturer just as eagerly proceeded to share his wealth of knowledge. To this day, I have never forgotten the principles acquired on that sunny Saturday afternoon, for they were the seeds of the knowledge from which the present work was born.

To open up the discussion and illustrate his interpretation of the crosses, Bériault began by creating three columns on the blackboard. To each, he assigned a title: Truth, Beauty, and Good and Evil. He turned to the participants and asked which of the crosses belonged to which header. The mutable signs were quickly and unanimously assigned to the Good and Evil group. Given the commonly understood dualistic nature of the cross, it was a bit of a giveaway. The identification of the remaining two crosses, however, proved to be more of a challenge, stirring up a lengthy yet highly revealing discussion regarding the significance of the Platonic trinity. Not being of a particularly scholarly turn of mind, it took some time before I was able to understand the essence of what was being proposed, but once I understood, it all seemed to make sense, and all without suffering through another reading of Plato's *Republic*!

Ever since that moment, I have continued to study and develop my understanding of the crosses, or *quadruplicities*, or *modes* as they are also known, and just as Arroyo's work on the elements, *Astrology, Psychology and the Four Elements*, opened up a whole new avenue for the interpretation of astrological factors, this radically new approach to the crosses seemed to open up whatever had remained hidden. Once I began to understand the fundamental characteristics of the crosses, it became much easier to evaluate the natal chart and to accurately identify transiting factors, as well as to recognize astrological phenomena in everyday life.

The crosses were the missing link. As my understanding of the dynamic nature of the crosses deepened, astrology took on a whole new rhythm, and as we shall see, this is exactly what the crosses are about—movement. Over the years, I began to recognize the crosses in peoples' speech patterns, in the style of their actions, in their methods of self-expression, in the words they chose to express what was on their minds or in their hearts, in the manner in which they carried themselves into a room, and in how they related with others.

The crosses have become such an integral part of my language and tools of observation that some of this knowledge has spilled over to family and friends, so that even people with little or no astrological training are able to explain the motivations and actions of their own friends simply by knowing to which cross their Sun sign belongs. For example, some time ago, just after starting a philosophy course in college, my younger daughter mentioned that she thought that Descartes might be a cardinal sign, perhaps even a Libra. Having been exposed to astrology most of her life, Caroline naturally had a basic knowledge of the zodiac, although this was limited mainly to Sun sign astrology. She had based her deduction on the style of his ideology. An interesting observation, I thought, since I already knew that Descartes had the Sun in Aries, but a look at his chart revealed that Libra was the focal point of his five Aries planets.

I have also used the crosses when presenting lectures to various groups and organizations of people who have had no training in astrology. A simple breakdown of the participants into their cross groups (most people today know their Sun sign) allows people to become quickly aware of some fundamental differences between themselves and friends and family members. With very little training, a mutable person, for example, might then understand the passion that drives his cardinal buddy, or a fixed sign might make allowances for her mutable friend's need to rationalize her actions. The study of the crosses results in a classification of character types into three basic, yet fundamental and undeniably distinct groups.

I've always maintained a deep fascination for human nature. Maybe I'm a bit of a voyeur, maybe it comes from being an astrologer, or perhaps it's the other way around and a certain degree of voyeurism is a required element for becoming an astrologer.

In any case, I've enjoyed watching people at work and at play, in their experiences of joy and pain, through their successes and triumphs, as they stumble over obstacles and as they succeed against all odds. In the beginning, I would try to guess a person's sign, but would just as often pick up the Moon, the Midheaven, a stellium, or the Ascendant as I would the Sun's placement. But when I began to integrate the principles of the crosses within my astrological frame of reference, a whole new process of perception began to emerge, and charts started to come to life. Some examples will illustrate this point.

Several years ago, I took to observing John, one of the instructors at a dojo where I trained in karate. My natural astrological curiosity led me to wonder what sign he might be, and my mind set itself to solving the puzzle, leading me to first suspect a cardinal-sign influence. The manner in which he taught his classes, coloured by a powerful presence, boundless energy and drive, and the dedication and discipline he devoted to his martial art all pointed to the cardinal signs. Add to that the characteristic cardinal physical traits, the prominent forehead and cheekbones, and the receding hairline often seen in Aries males. However, there was also a certain mutable quality in the way he moved, a quick nervousness, and a particular facial feature that I have often observed in individuals marked by this cross: a pair of long creases that appeared on the sides of his mouth when he smiled, revealing long, separate mutable teeth, a common mutable-sign trait. Combined with a very Sagittarian-like square jaw, I found this picture to be complex and, despite all these indicators, could not readily settle on any one cardinal sign.

For a time I juggled Aries and Cancer, and then considered Libra, for the martial aspect, having found the air signs to be prominent in the charts of fighters and martial artists, in particular, Libra and Aquarius. I discarded Aries, for there was too much discipline and continuity—twenty years (more than thirty years at the time of publication of the first edition of this book) of constant training in one field, with no forays into other

INTRODUCTION

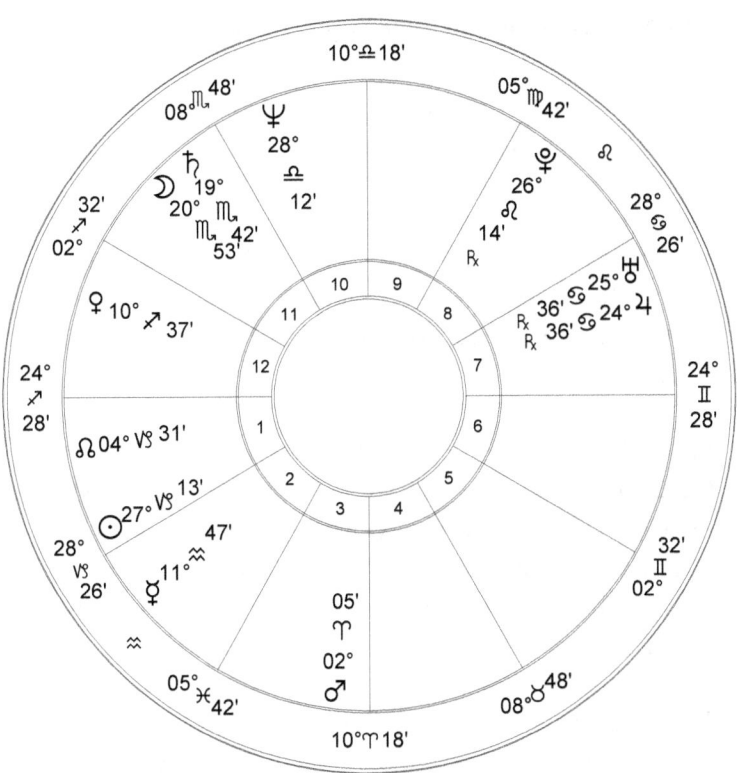

John

disciplines, but rather a definite loyalty to the style of the master; Aries might have tried other fields. Then I abandoned Cancer, for he lacked the sensitivity and nurturing of that sign; at least planetary placement in this sign was not outwardly evident. I threw out Libra, for the smile did not belong to this air sign, (Libra smiles are often wide, easy, and toothy), and also the projection of his personality was not openly and sociably Libran. Capricorn did not quite seem to fit the bill, because his nature was spontaneous and extremely independent and also very open to alternative health ideas.

Months later, I had the opportunity to draw up this person's chart and, lo and behold, discovered that he had the Sun in Capricorn opposed Jupiter and Uranus in Cancer, Mars in Aries, and a Libra Midheaven. Venus and the Ascendant were in Sagittarius. I was not surprised, and my observations were confirmed. It also became clear as to why I had difficulty settling with Capricorn, since the Sun was so strongly affected by Uranus and Jupiter, as well as being squared by Neptune in Libra!

In this example, the subject under observation remained obscured from view. Very late one night, a few winters ago, I heard a car pull up in front of my house. Curious as only a Moon in Aquarius can be, I drew back the blinds a crack and allowed myself to spy at the occupants of the late-model, imported sedan. My daughter and her driver, a young man from work, were calmly absorbed in what appeared to be a captivating discussion. It was a cold, icy night, and the driver had kept the motor running. While engaged in conversation, the driver shifted the car out of park a couple of times as though about to leave, only to shift it into park once more. Once or twice my daughter moved to open the door and each time was immediately reengaged in conversation. The driver's attention was evenly divided between the controls of his vehicle and the relational interaction at hand. Both seemed to be well under control—the vehicle and the guest in the car. The next morning I asked my daughter if her friend was a Virgo. She smiled, only half surprised and said that yes, he was.

Introduction

How did I know? I recognized the general nature of the cross and combined it with the finer elements of the sign. There was only one sign that embodied the quietly relational, environmentally aware, intimate nature expressed by this young man—Virgo.

Some time ago, I happened to catch a brief television interview with outspoken actor James Woods. The interviewer commented on his "bad-boy" image, to which the actor quickly and forcefully, but not without a certain air of boyish pleasure, responded, "I have zero image; I couldn't care less." Thinking that this response would naturally belong to a fixed sign, as concern for image belongs primarily to the cardinal signs, I proceeded to look up his birth data. I was surprised to discover that he was an Aries native, which did not fit my initial profile. On further thought, however, I understood that his ardent and self-satisfied response indicated someone who was enjoying the so-called "bad-boy" image, and that denial was only one way in which he chose to cultivate and even reinforce it.

Once a basic understanding of the crosses is acquired, the following exercise can be attempted. This is a wonderful way of testing and also of developing one's astrological know-how. Watch how people move, how they carry themselves, how they toss their hair, or how they step into a room. Observe their reactions and responses in everyday situations. Pay attention to the words people choose when they express themselves, especially in circumstances where the expression is spontaneous and natural. The following is a striking example of the crosses as they manifest in speech. The text below is an excerpt taken from an article written by Montreal astrologer Susan Kelly for "Directions." These interviews were conducted on the last day of the 1987 International Astrology Conference of the F.C.A. among astrologers who had attended the event. Several participants were asked to describe their experience of the conference, three of which are quoted below.

First person interviewed:
"I asked her why she thought the conference experience was important. 'It's important because there are so many different ways of looking at astrology, so many different views and methods and ideas. Conferences provide an excellent way to exchange our ideas and to get to know each other personally, to get to know the person behind the book, say. And when it's an international conference, you see people from abroad with whom you don't usually get a chance to talk.'"

Second person interviewed:
"'It's called "conference buzz." It's what you hear all around us. It's because we're all around so many Uranian types that too much electricity starts moving through us.' I pressed her for more details. Why would we want to get so charged up? 'Because we get off on the feeling.'"

Third person interviewed:
"We go through this conference experience, I think, for the sheer beauty of the experience."

To the trained observer, the language used in these three quotations is a truly remarkable reflection of each person's cross. The reader is invited to try to guess which interviewee is a cardinal, which is a fixed, and which is a mutable-sign native; the answers will be revealed in later chapters.

The following table will help determine to which cross group a person belongs; i.e., in which cross the Sun falls. For example, a person born on April 1 of any year will have the Sun in the sign Aries and will manifest some of the traits of the cardinal signs, while someone who is born on December 15 will have the Sun in Sagittarius and will express some mutable characteristics.

Cardinal	Fixed	Mutable
Spring/Summer	*Spring/Summer*	*Spring/Summer*
Aries (fire)	**Taurus** (earth)	**Gemini** (air)
MAR 21–APR 20	APR 21–MAY 20	MAY 21–JUN 20
Cancer (water)	**Leo** (fire)	**Virgo** (earth)
JUN 21–JUL 22	JUL 23–AUG 22	AUG 23–SEP 22
Fall/Winter	*Fall/Winter*	*Fall/Winter*
Libra (air)	**Scorpio** (water)	**Sagittarius** (fire)
SEP 23–OCT 22	OCT 23–NOV 21	NOV 22–DEC 21
Capricorn (earth)	**Aquarius** (air)	**Pisces** (water)
DEC 22–JAN 19	JAN 20–FEB 18	FEB 19–MAR 20

Astrologers and students of astrology will want to consult the complete chart for a more in-depth analysis of cross action in a chart. The extent to which a person will manifest the traits of a cross will be determined in part by the total number of astrological factors in that cross, including the planets, the Ascendant, and the Midheaven. For example, in the case of an Aries individual, the more planets there are in the cardinal signs, the more cardinal will be the nature of the person.

In the present work, when referring to a strong cross influence in a chart, this will usually indicate that there are four or more planets in one cross, reinforced by aspect configurations such as stelliums, squares, T-squares, Grand Crosses, position, and placement. However, it is not necessary for the Sun to be involved in the configuration for a cross influence to exist. In the case of the chart of entrepreneur Steve Jobs, whose chart is discussed later in this book, we find the Sun in the mutable sign Pisces with six planets distributed among the cardinal signs, giving a strong cardinal influence. In some charts, an aspect configuration (T-square, opposition, Grand Cross, etc.) that is strategically located, for example angular or elevated, can create a cross emphasis, while the natal Sun may not be included in the pattern.

Furthermore, the significance of the crosses goes beyond the placement of the Sun, planets, and angles in a natal chart. All points in a chart, including house cusps, can be considered by cross placement in making a complete horoscope delineation. For example, a person with a fixed sign on the cusp of the third house will think and communicate according to a specific, rather personal value set, whereas a person with a mutable sign on the third house is more likely to think and communicate according to a rationally deduced or an adopted set of rules and regulations.

We all have *something* in each of the crosses, and a study of these placements will reveal much about who we are and how we function. For those who have access to an astrologer or to a chart calculation service, it is recommended that you obtain information regarding the cross distribution in your chart. This will enable you to make a more thorough evaluation of your own character and personality traits.

Following is a list of names of people whose charts significantly reflect a specific cross emphasis. For the sake of making this information accessible to the nonastrologer, I have included in this list charts which have the Sun plus at least three other factors, including planets and the angles, in the same cross. The reader may find it interesting to refer to biographies and historical accounts of these people when reading through the descriptions of the individual crosses.

Cardinal sign individuals (Aries, Cancer, Libra, Capricorn)

Albert Schweitzer, René Descartes, Dwight Eisenhower, Richard Nixon, Ross Perot, Mary Baker Eddy, Friedrich Nietzsche, Michel de Notredame (Nostradamus), Nelson Rockefeller, Dr. Edward Bach, Jean Chrétien; writers Pearl S. Buck, Barbara Cartland, Charles Baudelaire (eight cardinal planets), George Orwell, Rudyard Kipling; artists, musicians and entertainers Herbert Von

Introduction

Karajan, Claudio Abbado, Victor Borge, Henri Matisse, Jacques Brel, Charlie Chaplin, Harrison Ford.

Fixed sign individuals (Taurus, Leo, Scorpio, Aquarius)

Martha Stewart, Franklin D. Roosevelt, Oprah Winfrey, Bill Clinton, Hillary Clinton, Angela Davis, George Lucas, Ted Turner, Charles Manson, Henry Ford, Adolf Hitler, Michele Sindona, Rudolph Valentino; writers James Joyce, George Bernard Shaw, Somerset Maugham, Bertrand Russell, Thomas Merton; artists, musicians and entertainers Johannes Brahms, Barbra Streisand, Pablo Picasso, Lucille Ball, Goldie Hawn, Julia Roberts, Rock Hudson.

Mutable sign individuals (Gemini, Virgo, Sagittarius, Pisces)

Albert Einstein, Michel de Montaigne, Brian Mulroney, Walt Disney, Queen Elizabeth I, Henry Kissinger, painter Toulouse Lautrec; writers Agatha Christi, Paolo Coelho, Sir Richard Burton, Ralph Waldo Emerson, William Butler Yeats; artists, musicians and entertainers, Ludwig Von Beethoven, Harry Connick Jr., Arthur Fiedler, Frank Sinatra.

As mentioned earlier, the crosses reveal themselves through the external manifestation of an individual's natural expression and so their traits can be easily observed in a person's words, accomplishments, achievements, and products. The reader may wish to compare the music of a cardinal composer with that of the other crosses, or the works of the painters or writers of different crosses. In observing and in listening, the crosses will quickly reveal themselves to you.

1
A Cross by Any Other Name

Qualities, quadruplicities, quadratures, modes, or types...it seems a necessary exercise just to sort through the various names given this division of the zodiac. The quadruplicities, as defined by astrologer Nicholas DeVore in his *Encyclopedia of Astrology*, "are the four signs which have the same quality; either cardinal, fixed or mutable." He further defines them by adding that "there are three types, or qualities...the Cardinal or Initiative signs, the Fixed or Executive signs and the Mutable or Deductive signs. As there are four in each, these are known as the Quadruplicities." Astrologers Marion March and Joan McEvers in *The Only Way to Learn Astrology* teach that "we can...divide the twelve signs of the zodiac into three groups of four signs each; the signs in each group have certain *qualities* in common. Each group has a distinct mode of operating in life. The qualities, or *quadruplicities* are..."

Although of common usage, the terms *type* and *quality* do not quite convey the intrinsically dynamic nature of the crosses, especially as they are revealed in speech and action, as intimated in the introduction of the current work. In fact, the term *quality* is at the very least a vague description and at worst a misleading

Astrological Crosses

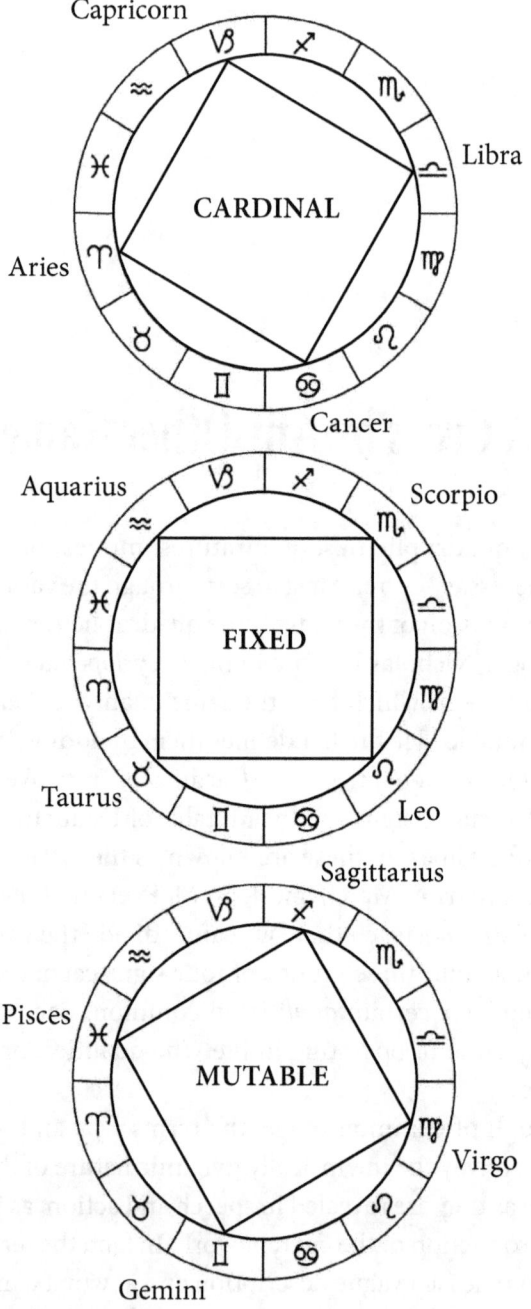

characterization of the crosses, because there are positive manifestations of each cross as well as destructive and harmful manifestations, as will be shown in the chapters that follow. A *quality* is generally perceived as a positive attribute, such as generosity, kindness, caring or a sense of humour, while in the full range of human experiences, the crosses can manifest less laudable traits, such as zealotry, cruelty, and indifference. But, as pointed out by March and McEvers, the crosses do indicate a distinct mode of operation.

The terms *quadruplicity* and *quadratures* refer to the relationship of the group to the number four—there are four signs in each cross grouping, just as the term *triplicity* refers to the three signs that belong to each of the four elements. There are also four signs per house grouping: angular, succedent, and cadent. However, the term *quadruplicity* does not seem to dignify the crosses with the uniqueness they deserve; they are much more than a structural division into three groups of four units.

In his classic work, *Astrology: How and Why it Works*, astrologer Marc Edmund Jones gives a thought-provoking, albeit somewhat esoteric, introduction to the crosses, even suggesting the existence of a process of individuation through manifestation in the crosses: "What the quadratures bring to the foreground of analysis... is the wholly individualistic way in which the given person stands up to experience in being himself, or the level upon which he characteristically enters upon or leaves a particular milieu of relationship... The cardinal, common (mutable) and fixed groupings of the signs—in their geometrical correspondence to the angular, cadent and succedent houses in that order—reveal the fundamentally dynamic recalcitrance of temperament, through the rather simple distinction between those... who (1) find the things at hand most interesting, (2) approach experience in mutual act or response with other people, and (3) meet the issues of their existence by following their own inner leading."

Jones' definition promises more for the crosses, implying the existence of a dynamic essence to be found within the crosses, a nature that is far more compelling than that represented by a mere "quality." Here we get a sense that the cross will actually motivate the native toward a process of individuation. Although individuation may not always be the goal of all motivation, there is much in the nature of each cross that will contribute to the nature of one's motivations.

A study of the actual structure derived from the angular relationships of the signs within a cross grouping gives us a better understanding of the dynamic nature of this sign division. Each sign in a cross is either in square aspect (a 90° relationship) or in opposition (a 180° relationship) to the other signs of the same group. Aries and Capricorn are in square aspect to each other, as are Libra and Cancer; Capricorn and Cancer are in opposition, as are Aries and Libra. Both the square and the opposition are challenging aspects and therefore hold a potential for growth, action, change, and transformation when expressed positively, or destruction and stagnation when a healthy outlet of expression has not been found.

By their fundamental structure, the crosses represent far more dynamic groups than do the elements. When connected together by aspect, each of the three signs of an element will form a Grand Trine; that is, they are in trine aspect to each other. For example, aspects drawn between planets at 15° of the signs Aries, Leo, and Sagittarius will form a triangle, or a fire Grand Trine. Trines represent the smooth, easy flow of energy, or the unchallenged exchange between two points, in this case, between three points. Trine aspects represent the talents and abilities toward which we turn when our need to be creative, proactive, or even reactive, supersedes our desire for maintenance and continuity. Trine-aspect configurations are used in our normal responses to life situations or just to go about our daily activities. In transit, trines can easily be taken for granted or even ignored. It has been my observation, through years of consultation work, that it is not the transiting trines that motivate an individual to take action

A Cross by Any Other Name

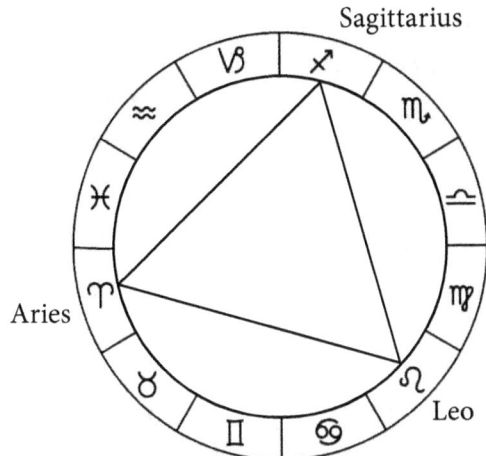

The Fire Signs (Fire Grand Trine)

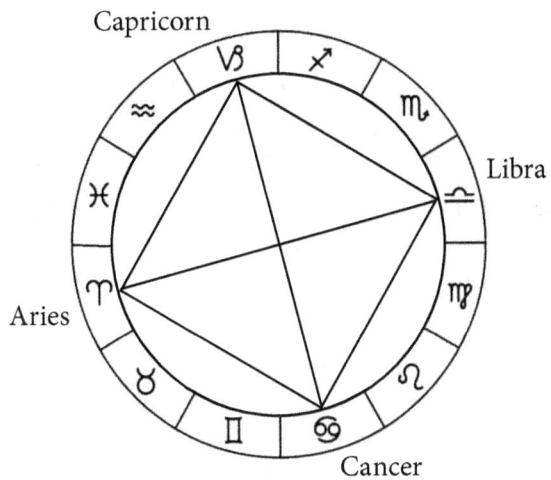

The Cardinal Cross

in life or to become creative and proactive, but rather the more challenging conjunctions, squares, and oppositions.

Challenging aspects, both natally and by transit, including progressions, solar arcs, solar returns, and midpoints, create the basic irritants that seem to be so necessary for bringing out creative and productive activity in many people, somewhat like when the oyster secretes nacre to coat a foreign object that has made its way inside its shell. Just as the oyster will create a pearl, we can create better lives for ourselves by bringing out and exercising our talents and special abilities. In general, people don't move unless they, for some reason, must. Without the challenging aspects, without the energy of the crosses, there would be little motivation to surpass our current condition.

Charts containing a lack of challenging aspects tend to be reflected in an easy and uncomplicated existence. Charts containing a healthy abundance of challenging aspects are reflected in the lives of individuals who are moved to go beyond the normal boundaries of common existence, for good or for ill. The popular expression "Necessity is the mother of invention" clearly illustrates this process. An individual who possesses a challenging configuration in his chart is likely to attempt to resolve the associated irritating factors in his life; an individual with an under challenged chart is likely to use a more passive approach to life situations. Note that other structural factors besides the hard aspects, such as sign placement and positioning, can generate stress in a chart.

Trines tend to placate, normalize, and stabilize, a necessary part of the process of growth and unfolding without which there would be no integration of experience or assimilation of knowledge. However, trines, in and of themselves, do not create the challenging environment that is essential to causing a person to actually take action. For example, an opposition of transiting Saturn to the ruler of the Midheaven might result in a loss of employment; yet the discomforting fear, insecurity and disappointment of this same opposition might be sufficient to provoke the individual to stand back and reevaluate (opposition) his career situation and, from there, take the necessary action, often based on the talents inherent in the chart as indicated in part by the trines. The reality check thus imposed by Saturn's transit might reveal to the native that he has long undervalued his abilities and must now make a choice to assume a level of responsibility that better reflects his abilities. In such a case, a difficult situation, as indicated by this "hard" transit, would have led to a desirable outcome.

If the transit had been a trine from Saturn, the situation would have been perceived as being far less compromising, and probably more as a positive opportunity to take advantage of experience and to assume additional responsibility. The result may seem similar, but the process is quite different; in the case of the opposition, the native is faced with a challenge that must be overcome, whereas in the case of the trine, the native simply goes along with the opportunity. Alternatively, with the trine aspect, the native could just as easily choose to forego the opportunity if no need for extra work, responsibility, or effort is experienced; whereas with the hard aspect, some form of action is generally required or at times even forced upon the native. There is a greater lesson learned with the opposition experience than with the trine experience.

While each member of an elemental group also shares the same polarity—for example, the three fire signs Aries, Leo and Sagittarius are also all of the yang, or masculine, polarity—each cross contains two yin, or feminine, signs, and two yang, or masculine, signs. For example, the cardinal cross counts the masculine signs Aries and Libra as well as the feminine signs Capricorn and Cancer. As well as being related to each other by dynamic aspects (squares and oppositions), the signs in a cross are further polarized by the confrontation of yin (negative or feminine) versus yang (positive or masculine) energies. When the cardinal signs Aries and Capricorn are linked by a square aspect, for instance, a further element of conflict is brought into play:

Astrological Crosses

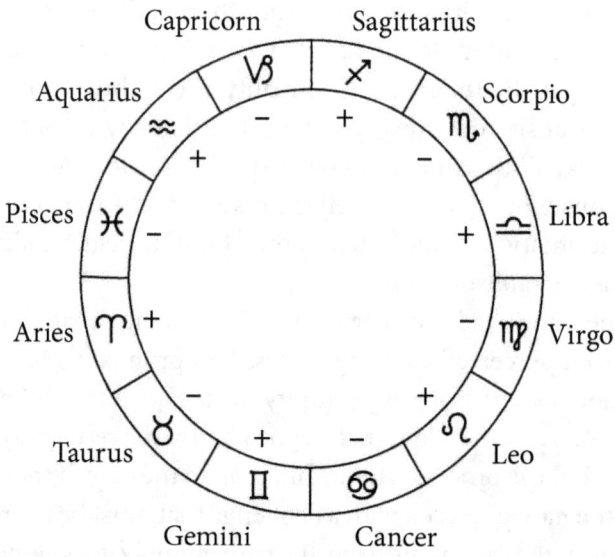

The Polarities: Yin (–) Yang (+)

Yin/feminine Signs
Taurus, Cancer, Virgo, Scorpio, Capricorn, Pisces

Yang/masculine Signs
Aries, Gemini, Leo, Libra, Sagittarius, Aquarius

the daring and bold outer self-expression and manifestation of the yang sign Aries versus the cautious, introverted, responsible, survival-oriented yin sign Capricorn. Planets in the yang sign Leo squaring planets in the yin sign Scorpio pit bold self-expression (Leo) against a need to preserve a sense of inner validation or integrity (Scorpio).

Another aspect that needs to be considered when attempting to understand the impact of angular relationships between planets and signs is the expansionary process that unfolds with the natural progression from the first to the last of the signs of the zodiac. This may be easier to perceive by imagining the zodiac from Aries to Pisces as though it were a spiral staircase instead of a closed wheel. As one climbs the stairs, one's perspective on events below changes. A similar change of perspective occurs in the natural progression of the signs. The spiral connotes movement, a flow of energy from one level to the next, giving a gradual increase in complexity of nature from Aries to Taurus to Gemini, etc. In Aries, there is singleness of purpose, centred around a personal and often immediate impulse; in Taurus, the focus is on direct experience and the satisfaction that it provides; in Gemini, we indulge in self-discovery through an exploration of the environment; in Cancer, purpose expands to include family members; in Leo, outlets are sought to externalize and express personal experience; and in Virgo, relationships are established for the purposes of ensuring the survival of one and all.

In the first six signs, commonly referred to as the *personal signs*, or the spring and summer signs, there appears a process of growth from a single-person-centred perspective (Aries to Gemini) to the beginnings of a community-based cooperative awareness (Cancer to Virgo). In the remaining six signs, referred to as the *social signs*, or the fall and winter signs, this perspective continues to expand, with Libra acting as a polarization force for the person-centred Aries, making "the other" a significant part of the equation of life; in Scorpio, the resources of others will be considered in addition to personal resources; in Sagittarius, the learning experience is expanded and organized into various systems and made available to the community; in Capricorn, the structuralisation process of society is completed by the implementation of a governing body; in Aquarius, humanity reaches the fullness of its self-expression and seeks to explore unchartered territory; and in Pisces, all knowledge and experience are combined into one complete, transcendental experience to be shared by the collective awareness. Note that this analogy could have been approached from many different aspects; this is only one way of connecting the signs to each other. The reader is invited to trace other possible developmental lines, using varying facets of the signs.

Given the expanding perspective inherent in the zodiacal spiral, the relationships between the signs of a cross are further vitalized in their contacts with each other, so that the self in Aries must consider family in Cancer, which must find balance in its partnerships and associations in Libra and then find meaning and purpose in a worldly function in Capricorn. The sense of self-worth of Taurus will be tested as it shows the world what it values in Leo, only to be purified in Scorpio and then taken beyond the boundaries of the common experience to be further tested in Aquarius. Gemini's interaction with the outside world will be focused on cooperation and survival in Virgo, which will then grow to include the broader hierarchies of society in Sagittarius and then be released into the universal networks of Pisces. The same principle holds true when taken in reverse order; for example, when confronted by Leo, Aquarius must take into account the very real feelings of the individual (Leo) despite his or her vision of a grander, more understanding humanity (Aquarius). Alternatively, what is good for the family (Cancer) may not necessarily be what the individual (Aries) needs.

In providing an appropriate appellation for this division of the zodiac into three groups of four signs, it is essential to consider the inherent tensions in the relationships between each of the signs, from gender dichotomy to hard-aspect configuration.

The Social Signs, or Fall and Winter Signs
Libra, Scorpio, Sagittarius, Capricorn, Aquarius, Pisces

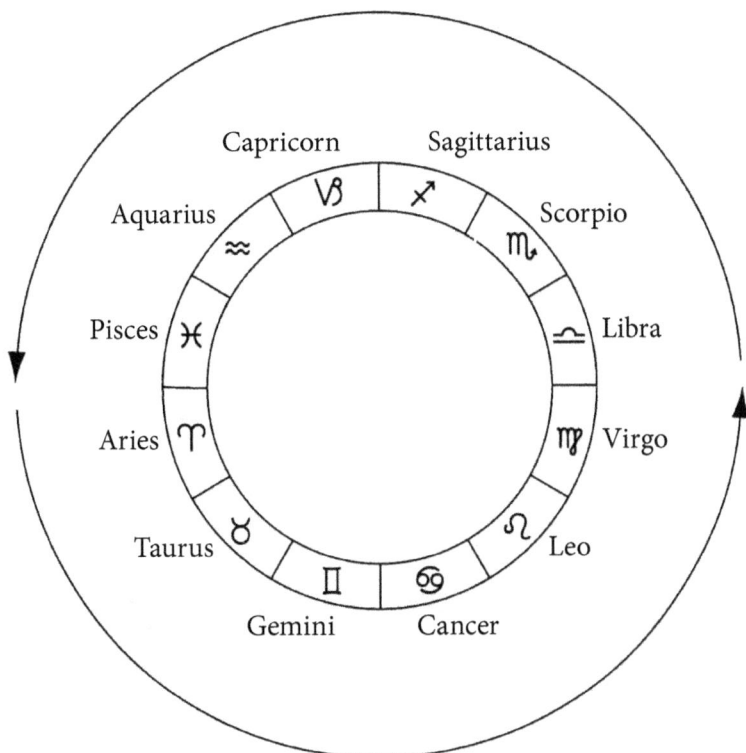

The Personal Signs, or Spring and Summer Signs
Aries, Taurus, Gemini, Cancer, Leo, Virgo

Just as the term *elements* aptly describes the fire, earth, air, and water groupings, it now appears evident that the term *crosses* appropriately reflects the dynamic structure of the threefold division of the zodiac into the cardinal, fixed, and mutable signs.

2

The Cardinal Cross

Aries, Cancer, Libra, Capricorn

"I say to you today, my friends, that in spite of the difficulties and frustrations of the moment, I still have a dream. It is a dream deeply rooted in the American dream. I have a dream that one day this nation will rise up and live out the true meaning of its creed: We hold these truths to be self-evident: that all men are created equal... I have a dream today. I have a dream that one day every valley shall be exalted, every hill and mountain shall be made low, the rough places will be made plain, and the crooked places will be made straight, and the glory of the Lord shall be revealed, and all flesh shall see it together."[1]

—Dr. Martin Luther King, Jr.

---

1. Delivered on the steps of the Lincoln Memorial in Washington D.C., August 28, 1963.

The Power of the Dream

The cardinal signs are the dreamers of the zodiac. Okay, let me explain...I can hear the Capricorns grumbling already and the Librans warming up for an animated debate and the Cancers feeling unjustly disparaged and Aries...well...they've already dashed on to the next paragraph. Dreams do not come only in the impossible variety, they come in all sizes and shapes. In fact, dreaming is a very healthy and desirable activity that is part of the sometimes complex process in which we engage in order to define and achieve our life goals. Our dreams are often all that sustain us through the most trying of times. It is an activity that is naturally practised by young children until they are taught to grow up, to become reasonable and practical, and to deal with the issues at hand. There is a youthful hopefulness in those grown-ups who have managed to maintain some of this childhood ability to dream. As we shall see, dreams vary greatly in nature and also in realization potential, from the possible to the impossible. An impracticable dream is likely to remain in the realm of fantasy, an escape from reality, and will rarely lead to a significant accomplishment, whereas a realistic dream will nurture the spirit and provide hope and inspiration in times of difficulty and in the face of obstacles—these dreams become the stuff on which personal success is built.

When I encounter clients who are having difficulty finding a life direction, I ask them to try to recall what they dreamed of doing when they were young. They may stammer, blush, or become self-conscious and even embarrassed as I wait for them to reveal their long-buried, sometimes secret dreams. More often than not, they will remember their dream, and when they do, their eyes light up as though their soul had just received a wake-up call. This cardinal spark is that part of the force that drives us to move forward in life to complete the search for self, so that we may resolve our soul's quest in this lifetime. To dream is a vital function of becoming, an essential ingredient of being.

The Cardinal Cross

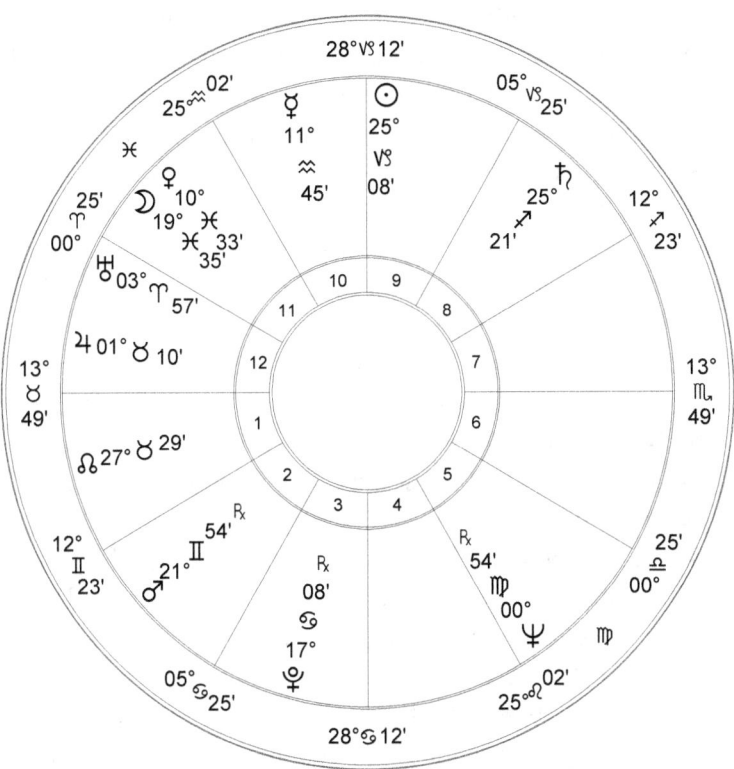

Dr. Martin Luther King, Jr.
January 15, 1929

Without the ability to dream, Mount Everest would not have been climbed, (Sir Edmund Hillary, one of the first two men to reach the summit of Mount Everest in 1953, has the Sun, Jupiter, Mars, and Pluto in the cardinal sign Cancer, as well as the Moon in Aries.), man would not have landed on the Moon, Kekulé would not have discovered the benzene ring (Okay, so that happened in an actual dream!), and airplanes would never have gotten off the ground; in fact, without vision, mankind would have taken far fewer steps forward. Dr. Martin Luther King's dream was based on his vision for mankind, a vision that reflected the very real need for all human beings to have equal rights, and with his Sun in the cardinal sign of Capricorn, he had the courage and personal power to stand tall and to express his convictions for all to hear.

Specialists today stress the importance of being able to reactivate the often lost, forgotten, buried, or even suppressed childhood ability to dream. Workshops abound where we can learn to envision a better life, to create new mental pictures for ourselves, to visualize the life we want to live. Lectures, tapes and videos by motivational speakers continue to be popular. Having a vision to guide us through life is an essential component of the development of a satisfactory and fulfilling life experience. But, a person does not have to be a visionary to be successful in life, one only has to be able to look beyond current circumstances. This is in essence what the cardinal cross provides, the ability to reach out, to see beyond that which is here now. Cardinal dreams are often born of instinct, feeling, and passion; they can stem from feelings of pain, loss, grief, or desperation. They are generally not based on a process, whether extensive or brief, of logic and reason, although they can be stimulated by such a process when the process is driven by a need.

In Bériault's discourse on the crosses, he assigned Truth to the cardinal cross, giving the following as an essential principle for the cardinal signs: *equating an idea to a reality, or making an idea conform to reality*. This is the cross of hopefulness, of aspiring toward an ideal, of enriching the present with a dream for the future, and of hoping that this dream can one day be made real. It is the essential energy that drives us forward and charges us with the motivation and courage to overcome the difficulties we encounter in life. It is what keeps us climbing when the summit seems unattainable, it keeps us walking when the road seems to have disappeared, and it keeps us fighting even in the face of inevitable failure. Cardinal energy enriches us with the courage to stand up and try again after we have fallen; it enables us to keep trying despite our seeming failures.

> *"Ideals are like stars; you will not succeed in touching them with your hands. But like the seafaring man on the desert of waters, you choose them as your guides, and following them you will reach your destiny."*[2]
>
> —Carl Schurz

Dreams that can be translated into possible realities can be developed into workable plans; that is, dreams that are founded in a sufficient base of realism have a chance of becoming a reality. These dreams are what move visionaries to seek and achieve greatness. These are the dreams that ultimately lead to change. Although not all individuals will realize their dreams, it is sometimes the vision alone that keeps many people alive, it keeps most cardinals sufficiently motivated to keep moving forward and helps them leap out of bed in the morning, ready to face another day. Cardinal energy is a great driving force.

Cardinal individuals can for the most part buffer themselves against the unpleasant facets of the outside world, and of life if need be, by placing their dreams and sometimes delusions between themselves and the world. They can remain secure for a long time with the belief that some day their dream will come true, that things were meant to get better for them, that they are somehow destined to leave their mark on the world, and that

---

2. Carl Schurz (1829-1906), German-born U.S. senator. Excerpt from a speech delivered on April 18, 1859, in Boston, Massachusetts.

what they do, and who they are, is of significance in the overall scheme of things. Just as the capacity to dream can promote a healthy pace of forward movement through life, problems can arise when there is confusion between dream and reality. A dream that cannot be accomplished, either because it is based on an idea that is completely unrealistic in scope or is built on a faulty foundation, will fall into the realm of fantasy and, when perpetuated, can contribute to delusional behaviour.

Cardinals can be quite zealous in the expression of their ideals and will sometimes try very hard to make reality conform with their ideal. Here is how a friend of mine once described a situation he was experiencing concerning his boss: "He is trying to make reality fit his understanding." I asked if he knew his boss' sign, thinking that this was very much a typical cardinal problem. "His birthday is April 8," was his immediate reply. Cardinals can become so caught up in their idea that they sometimes lose touch with the very reality into which they are attempting to incarnate their idea, a frustrating experience indeed for the cardinal person who is feeling the pressures of accumulating unmanifested energy, and equally frustrating for anyone in the immediate vicinity who must endure the consequences. This is the cross of living according to an ideal, according to a set of valued principles or laws. Taken to the extreme, or used in a misguided way, cardinal energy can forcefully impose its ideas or ideology on the environment, regardless of the needs or desires of that environment. The "power trip" is typically a cardinal manifestation, where one person's ideals are lorded over another, sometimes at great cost to the other person.

The cardinal signs are more likely than the fixed or mutable signs to be drawn to causes, movements, and cults, especially if these display plenty of gloss, ceremony, glitter, and panache. This can range anywhere from obedience to the laws of an established form of religion to the adoption of more radical sociopolitical views. They will be attracted more for their desire to be surrounded by energy and movement, as is usually the case with an organized cause, than by a need to exchange and communicate with other people (mutable) or a need to share their innermost values (fixed).

The idea of fame, glory and worldly fortune appeals to the cardinals, and although many will attempt to achieve a certain level of notoriety for themselves, there are those who, perhaps by virtue of their social position or of their limited self-image, will remain content just to work or to remain in close proximity to someone who manifests this level of energy and personal success. The more confident cardinal natives will want to have the whole ball of wax and go for the position that maximizes their experience. Motivational speakers and writers, as well as business, social, and political leaders, usually have a strong cardinal influence in their charts.

The extreme of the idealist is the zealot who will engage in fanatical actions stemming from the deeply ingrained influences of some form of religion, doctrine, belief, dogma, creed, philosophy, or school of thought. These are the militants, the fanatics, the tyrants, and the activists who consider themselves to be the "true believers," select members of the "one true faith." They can also adopt the extreme position of being willing to die for their adopted cause. There is no reasoning with people who have reached this state, only venting, and the only thing that might stop them in their endeavours, when things have gone too far, is an actual encounter with a person or representative of a higher authority and power. This can result in them falling back in line, for cardinals have a deep respect for, and fear of, power and authority.

While looking for an example to illustrate an aspect of the cardinal cross, I telephoned my brother Michael (nine fixed planets, zero cardinal, one mutable!) for a reference to a title of a book or movie with the word *glory* in it. He informed me that there were many. When I asked if he could give me a big name, he replied that he generally avoided anything with that word *glory* in it, no doubt a blatant reaction to the lack of cardinal energy in his own chart. I laughed and muttered something about not being surprised, given his cross configuration, to which he added, "Mommy will know, she reads books like that." This turned out to be true enough, indeed, and wouldn't you know it, although a mutable sign, Mommy just happens to have the Moon, Mercury, Venus, Saturn, Uranus, and Pluto in cardinal signs!

Somewhere in the balance between the zealot and the dreamer lies the "idea man" (or woman, of course). The cardinal cross carries the energy of the impulse, the original idea. In a concrete analogy, the planning and design phase of building a house would be considered the cardinal phase, at which time a blueprint is drafted and the required energy, money, and interest are summoned in order to get the project off the ground. Contacts are made, plans are set into motion, and the project begins to take shape. The planning phase of any project is usually a very exhilarating time, filled with hope and anticipation, and sometimes replete with a promise of personal success and, yes, potential "glory." It is a positive time where, above all else, the goal or the finished product is considered. Minds, bodies, hearts, and souls are filled with energy as the various dynamics of the project are set into motion.

Action will take cardinal individuals out of the realm of the idea, whether dream or fantasy, and bring them one step closer to the achievement of the goal. In bringing the dream or idea into the realm of the real and the actual, a goal has been achieved. It now becomes time to find or manifest another idea; hence, the tendency of some cardinal natives to appear to be always on the go, perpetually in motion, always moving from one project to another. They have an inner need to experience movement, and their motivation is not always born out of logical deduction; it is more of an inner impulse, so at times their actions may appear to be wayward or even absurd. Cardinal signs may occasionally need to be reminded of the importance of enjoying life for the moment, to once in a while stop just long enough to acknowledge the wonderful smell of the roses before going off to build a water garden.

The Voice of Authority

Given their natural leadership abilities, cardinal-sign individuals will generally tend to reach for positions in which they can manifest a certain level of power and authority. When they have not assumed or reached a position of authority of their own, they seem to gravitate toward persons of authority and power as a way of finding their way to their own position of power. They will even encourage this authority, support it, nurture it, as though they in some vicarious way can benefit from it. For example, a cardinal student will bring gifts to a respected teacher, and will be supportive of this person of authority. Cardinals will seek references from books written by persons of authority in their fields. They will accept the word of persons in authority until they have developed a sufficient sense of their own authority. Sometimes they will defer to the authority of another as a means of avoiding the pressure of being their own voice of authority, partly due to a lack of self-confidence, and partly due to fear of the reprimands associated with disrespect of the laws of authority. Whether out of fear or out of respect for authority, there is definitely an awareness of its power and influence.

Idealistic, but without sufficient power of their own, the weaker cardinals, lacking in self-confidence, will seek out strong individuals who hold definite ideals of their own. The more powerful the ideas, the person, and the presentation of these ideas, the more likely is the cardinal to adopt this line. They will show support and respect, and may even be willing to sacrifice themselves for the superior cardinal who appears to hold the virtues that they will never manifest. A "herd" or "groupie" mentality can grow from this need to associate with a person of ideals and power, sometimes allowing such individuals to follow in the footsteps of a leader of questionable values, morals, or even credibility.

At times, a certain naive blindness, sometimes voluntary, sometimes not, can cause all rational and objective thought or intervention from friends and family members to be ignored and even denied. The astrologer should be aware of this tendency, as cardinal clients can be rather vulnerable to suggestion during consultation, the more so if the astrologer has already proven his or her abilities. Once the astrologer has been accepted as a person of knowledge and authority, cardinal individuals are likely to consult during times of crisis more often than individuals of the other crosses. As it is the responsibility of the astrologer to guide and inform clients rather than to have power and authority over them or over their life affairs, it is important to recognize that cardinal clients, in times of crisis, can expect the astrologer to assume this power and even make a decision in their stead. This is an easy trap into which some may fall, especially when the astrologer cares for and wants to help the client.

Given the passion with which they hold on to their convictions, cardinal-sign individuals are often perceived as the right persons to hold positions of leadership and authority. Once in such a position, they will do their utmost to gain and maintain the respect of their peers, their subordinates, and especially their superiors. They are hard working, passionately devoted, loyal, and generous with their time and energy. They make great role models for young people, and those working close to them will naturally thrive as they bask in the warmth of their energy and enthusiasm. Cardinals derive a sense of pleasure from the power they hold and wield, and will do what they can to augment and maintain it.

In a critical situation, the cardinal sign can, if necessary, pull rank and claim a right based on his position of authority. They can use phrases such as, "I'm your mother...I'm your father...I'm your boss..." believing that their superior rank entitles them to the respect and obedience they are demanding. Being that cardinal signs have an innate understanding of the nature of power and can express it in a natural, believable manner, their authority is likely to be respected by others. They might even holler and expect obedience and respect for no reason other than they believe that they deserve it and have earned it, in which case the bark is worse than the bite. A profoundly disturbed cardinal, harbouring deep-seated anger and power issues, who desires power but, for many possible reasons, has not found a way or a place in which to manifest it appropriately, will have a real bite to follow that bark, and one would be wise to step back when the gates of wrath tear themselves open.

If cardinals signs do not hold a sufficient level of authority, they are likely to call on someone who does in order to resolve the situation or problem at hand, for in the cardinal way of thinking, things must keep moving, goals must be met, and plans must be carried through. They will not hesitate to call the boss, the department head, the president, the chief, the doctor, the police, the clergy, a person holding public office, or whoever the appropriate authority person might be, given the situation. Under normal circumstances, in a world of unlimited resources, there is usually something or someone out there who will provide a solution or an answer.

A Life of Impact

When considered in relation to the natural cycles of the Earth's yearly journey around the Sun, the cardinal cross is associated with the months that bring in the changes of season: Aries proclaims the rebirth of nature in spring, Cancer wraps us in the lush warmth of summer, Libra presents an autumn tapestry of colour, and Capricorn ushers in the challenges of winter. In the birth chart, the cardinal signs are associated with the angles: first house (or Ascendant), fourth house (IC), seventh house (Descendent) and tenth house (MC). In this affiliation the cardinal cross reveals a powerful energy of movement and direction; in the cardinal cross is found our ability to move ourselves and the world around us to manifest our goals and to realize our dreams and visions.

The need for movement in the cardinal signs is born of a need to experience sensory, emotional and/or mental stimulation. Cardinals are generally on-the-go types who are in pursuit of as many goals or objectives as are humanly possible, and who are usually inclined to expend the energy that is required to maintain their momentum. A typical example of this type of behaviour today is the superwoman: She is a career dynamo, usually holding a position of some importance, an involved parent, participating in car-pooling and other activities for the benefit of her children, and is sometimes even involved in community activities as well as being a devoted spouse. If you're tired just reading this, your cardinal energy probably needs a boost; ask superwoman if she would have it any other way and she'll likely tell you flat-out, "No-way! But I sure wouldn't say no to a vacation!"

Arlette is a successful business woman in her fifties who travels much for her business and is generally always on the go. Her idea of a vacation is a dogsled trek in the Arctic, looking for penguins in Iceland, or a nature adventure in the Galapagos. Here is a woman who is constantly occupied and who has attained a healthy and very rewarding balance of activities between her personal life and her professional responsibilities.

In order to begin to realize a dream, the cardinal signs sometimes have to suffer some level of pain, or some amount of aggravation; they must *feel* the need to move and to change their life circumstances. Feeling is as essential to the life experience of the cardinal signs as is breathing. I once inquired of a cardinal friend how it was that he could pursue a love interest that he knew had no hope of ever coming to fulfilment and that caused him immeasurable pain. The response to my query was quick and simple: "But it makes me feel so alive." Sometimes cardinals would rather suffer pain than not feel anything at all. Action, movement, goals, ambitions, challenges... cardinal signs thrive on them and they will actively seek them out. For some strong cardinal types, the bigger the need for ego gratification, the bigger the fuss, the noise, and the hoopla!

Cardinal energy, by its dynamic nature, must find an avenue of expression. A healthy and very energetic sixty-nine-year-old woman with six cardinal planets explained to me how she found it interesting that with age, as much as she wanted to maintain the same pace and stamina as was her usual expression, her body had begun to dictate otherwise. Not so long ago, this vigorous grandmother used to easily climb a certain fence on a rugged shortcut route with which she had become familiar over the years, whereas now she was disappointed to discover that she no longer had the physical strength and agility to get herself over the same hurdle.

The cardinal signs are the movers, the shakers, and the noise makers of our society. They are the leaders of movements and the champions of causes, driven by their passions and motivated by the force of their convictions to make their dreams happen. They are the mouthpieces, the frontrunners, and are often given positions of leadership and authority such as general manager, CEO, foreman, chairman, president, director, etc. Cardinal-sign individuals are found in prominent positions more often than are their fixed and mutable counterparts, a fact that sometimes reflects more on their need for visibility and power than on their actual abilities and competence. In its drive for manifestation, the cardinal sign is motivated by a need to feel the force of its own power through movement or participation in a plan of substance.

Bruce, a middle-aged man with the Sun, Mars and Uranus in Cancer, and Saturn and Neptune in Libra, once recounted tales of days gone by as a professional football player. He laughed as he recalled what he used to tell his coach before a game to get himself geared up for the event: "Coach, hit me, hit me, coach," he would say, "I play better when it hurts!" An Aries friend with four planets in cardinal signs, plus an Aries Midheaven, gets a big kick out of eating *spoonfuls* of wasabi whenever he goes out for sushi. Anyone who has had the pleasure of eating sushi knows that eating a spoonful of wasabi (an extremely hot Japanese horseradish) is akin to sucking on a bowlful of jalapeno peppers! This person also enjoys chomping on coffee beans while driving long distances. He likes the rush it gives him. Another cardinal friend of mine once found himself in an animated debate with a fixed-sign friend, arguing the merits of eating a chocolate bar all in one mouthful, describing how the impact of the pleasure was greater with a mouth packed with the candy rather than with individual bites. In contrast, the fixed-sign person preferred to prolong the pleasure with as many decent mouthfuls as possible.

The cardinal need for movement is often externalized in such a way as to maximize the impact of the sensation by involving others in the experience. Cardinal signs are generally concerned with the effect their actions will have on their environment and may even tailor their actions accordingly. A cardinal client, when questioned about her deeper motivations, indicated that she would like to maybe open up a health centre or spa, so that after she dies, she will have left something behind, and perhaps have in some way influenced the world. Another client, a twenty-seven-year-old man, wanted to do more in life than just run an already successful business. He wanted to make a difference in the world, to participate in activities directed at youth in the streets and develop drug treatment programs for these youth. These are natural cardinal inclinations, and they form an important part of the motives behind these individuals' life choices.

By now you may have guessed the cross of the astrologer who, when asked why she thought the conference experience was important, replied: "It's called 'conference buzz.' It's what you hear all around us. It's because we're all around so many Uranian types that too much electricity starts moving through us." I pressed her for more details. Why would we want to get so charged up? "Because we get off on the feeling." This woman is clearly a native of the cardinal signs, more precisely, Capricorn.

The cardinal signs are the peacocks of the world, and, as in nature, the males of the species can oftentimes be found to outshine the females with their bold style and fashion flair. I knew a man of medium stature, not more than five foot five, with five cardinal planets in his natal chart, who felt entirely comfortable wearing a three-piece suit including suspenders, with the whole look topped off with an oversized fedora, to an event where many wore jeans and sports jackets. A Taurus woman, with six fixed planets, was amused to discover that her Capricorn boyfriend, six cardinal planets, not only kept a pharmacy filled with all manner of facial and skin care products, but that he actually had streaks put into his hair at the hairdresser. "That's what women do!" she exclaimed. Cardinal men are not averse to experimenting with their looks and will go so far as colouring and even streaking their hair. A very stout comedienne once came on stage wearing a long, bright, colourful dress and unabashedly declared, "If you can't hide it, decorate it!" She was making a very cardinal statement. Cardinal women will often extend their sense of flair to include the family, ensuring that their children are appropriately attired and that the home is a reflection of their ideals.

Several years ago, I was telling my friend Linda, a lovely lady with the Sun and Mercury in Aries opposed Jupiter in Libra, about my plans to present my astrology services to business clients. Linda is a colour and image consultant and a professional makeup artist, as well as a highly experienced esthetician. She had already counselled me on personal style, colour, and makeup, and her immediate and spontaneous response was, "Oh, all dressed up in a suit, you'll look great! You shouldn't have any problems." We had not been discussing my wardrobe at the time, but I had to smile when I recognized the quick (Aries) and obviously cardinal response: If you look good, you'll have the desired impact and this should contribute to your success. It's a simple formula, if you have sufficient cardinal energy and not too much fixed or mutable energy to run interference!

Betty is an Aries with Libra rising, with four cardinal planets including Mars and Neptune in Libra, who owns and runs a trophy and gift shop. The cardinal signs provide the drive, energy, and entrepreneurship that have led her to develop a very successful business. When she presents herself at business networking meetings, she uses the following tagline: "An engraved product leaves a lasting impression." This is a very cardinal representation of her business.

Cardinals can also rely on their charm, of which they tend to have plenty, in their interactions with the world, from the personal and intimate to the social and worldly. Who can resist the boyish charm of martial artist-turned-actor, Libra native Jean-Claude VanDamme or actor Robert Downey, Jr., an Aries native? The term *charismatic* is often used to describe cardinals such as the late Canadian Prime Minister Pierre Elliot Trudeau. What they might occasionally lack in common sense or erudition, cardinals certainly make up for with energy, style, and charm. They are adept at making an impact when they enter a room, are quick to be surrounded by admirers, and will usually find their way to the hub of the action. They are genial hosts and will fuss and fret until they are satisfied that all your needs have been met and you are enjoying yourself as much as they are. They take their social responsibilities just as seriously as they do their professional ones, and will valiantly protect and care for those who are entrusted to them.

A Capricorn woman with eight cardinal planets (the Sun, Moon, Mercury, Mars, Saturn, Venus, Neptune, and Jupiter) found herself in a trying situation during a business networking breakfast when, unexpectedly, a rather large chunk of her front tooth broke off. As members rose in turn to introduce themselves to the group, her anxiety mounted. She laboured over having to stand in front of a group of thirty strangers and present herself with a gaping hole in her smile. Finally, she approached the moderator, excused herself, and quietly left the meeting, too uncomfortable to face the group with such an unpresentable appearance.

How might the other crosses have responded in a similar situation? The fixed signs might have pushed himself to go through with the meeting, no less self-conscious, and would have suffered the embarrassment while promising himself to never eat breakfast in a restaurant again. Fixed signs feel more comfortable with problem situations once they think they have a solution. While "never eating in a restaurant again" is an extreme and impracticable solution for this situation and does not even address the problem of the broken tooth, the fixed sign will always feel somehow empowered with the knowledge that *something* can and will be done.

A mutable individual might have reacted differently, perhaps looking for the humour in the situation, or perhaps finding a tale to tell of an even more embarrassing moment. This is not to say that the mutable sign is devoid of any feelings of self-consciousness; in fact, the mutable may be even more self-conscious than the cardinal and the fixed in a social context, but mutables can be slightly more at ease (though not necessarily less shy) in social situations as they are more flexible in their interactions with others and can call on a number of possible responses in any given social exchange. As we will soon see, the mutables are more socially agile than the fixed or the cardinal signs.

Look to the cardinal aspects of your chart for sources of motivation, energy, and inspiration. A cardinal Ascendant normally provides a fair amount of personal charm and charisma; a cardinal Midheaven will provide ambition and drive; a cardinal house cusp will point to an area of life that could give you clues about your inner dream as well as offering avenues of expression for your personal power. A cardinal fifth house, for example, gives energy and imagination to the creative process. In the absence of cardinal planetary placement, look at the cardinal house cusps for areas of activity that might provide inspiration, stimulus, and excitement.

Growing up Cardinal

Cardinal children are busy, active children; the world is their stage, and their experience of life is their personal drama. They need to feel the impact of their own power on their surrounding environment. These children thrust himself outwards and on to the world, relishing each experience, drawing from it all possible sensation. They are the most likely to engage in power struggles with parents, teachers, and authority figures. If they are surrounded by controlling, powerful adults, they may find it necessary to temporarily submit to the adults' power in order to survive. But as they mature, they are very likely to lash out in an attempt to assume power of their own. These children respond to power and authority, and they will test a parent's power to the limit. If you are up to the test, you will be respected; if not, these children will attempt to destroy your authority.

One summer, my daughter held a job as monitor in a summer camp for children and, having Mercury in Gemini in the fifth house, she found this to be a thoroughly enjoyable occupation. She found the youngsters to be quite endearing, in particular one seven-year-old boy who had taken to sitting next to her during her lifeguarding shifts. He said that he preferred her company to that of the other children in the pool, adding that he just liked to "hang out" with her. I asked if she knew what sign he was, suggesting that he was probably a cardinal sign, since he sought the company of a person of authority, and furthermore Cancer was a likely possibility, since he chose a female idol over a male. She agreed that this made sense and made a mental note of finding out his birth date. Not surprisingly, he turned out to be a Cancer.

It is important for the healthy development of cardinal children that there be a positive relationship with a person in authority other than a parent, such as a "big brother," an older friend, a teacher, coach, neighbour, or relative. Exposure to the healthy and positive application of personal power and authority will allow cardinal children to develop their own power. It is also important for these children to develop positive outlets for the expression of their personal power. One way is to provide them with the opportunity to exercise authority through gradually increasing responsibilities such as feeding the cat or walking the dog. These responsibilities must provide a valid challenge for them, for they will know if you are just playing with them. On the other hand, the challenges must not be so great as to discourage them right from the start.

Cardinal children who are not given the opportunity to develop a sense of power will, later in life, struggle with feelings of inadequacy through powerlessness. They may grow to envy or resent persons in positions of authority, which could in turn lead to problems with bosses and difficulties in holding down a job. They may outright refuse to assume responsibility for themselves and their life in general. In order to feel balanced and healthy, cardinal individuals do need to get a feel for their own personal power.

3

The Fixed Signs

Taurus, Leo, Scorpio, Aquarius

"Because a man does not state in so many words the reason that leads him to some action, it does not follow that he is led by no reason. Because he does not even know the reason, it does not follow that there is none. And giving himself one, he may be again mistaken and give the wrong one."
—W. Somerset Maugham

The Power of Perception

When I first read the above quotation, it struck a chord deep within my spirit. Finally, I thought, as I savoured the words, someone who showed a true understanding of how the fixed signs work. I was even more pleased to discover that Somerset Maugham was a native of the sign Aquarius, with five planets in the fixed signs, including the Sun and Moon. These simple words had expressed something that I had for a long time felt, but was unable to articulate clearly, simple words that had the effect of liberating the spirit, of lightening the load, and of erasing the burden of conformity and expectation. This statement, I felt, held the essence of the fixed signs.

The standard definitions of the fixed signs reveal them to be, at best, steadfast, determined, and reliable, and at worst, stodgy, dull, and boring. The fixed cross relates to reality as it has been experienced in the past and as it is perceived in the present moment. In this way, the strongly fixed individual can be more connected to immediate circumstances or to the present than are natives of the other two crosses. In this relationship to perceived reality, the fixed signs find the strength and power of their convictions. "This is the way I see it, this is the way it is." To the fixed signs, perception is reality and reality is perception.

The fixed signs are, in fact, the creators, the developers, the producers of the zodiac, and are at their best when involved in an activity that they consider to be of value. Although for the most part productive, fixed signs can find themselves trapped in the immediately perceived reality, and when this occurs, they are unable to be creative and can be inflexible in their attitudes and actions. When not actively involved in an endeavour that appeals to their interests, values, and tastes, fixed-sign individuals can be indifferent, intolerant, unmotivated, introverted, isolating, uncooperative, unproductive, and even destructive. If they are stuck in a rut of dull, day-to-day routine, they can come to believe that this is the only reality that is possible for them. When this occurs, they develop a sense of worthlessness and can consider themselves to be stupid and untalented. Bit by bit, they then sink further and further into a pit of despair.

A fixed sign with nothing of significance to do, or in the face of an unresolvable problem, can become, in effect, completely inert. Some might call this lazy, but *disengaged* would be a more appropriate term to describe the state that causes the fixed sign to become unproductive. The only way out of such a state is for the person to reconnect with something of personal interest and value. Fixed signs will usually be found progressing steadily, even slowly, on a path of personal satisfaction, but at times they may

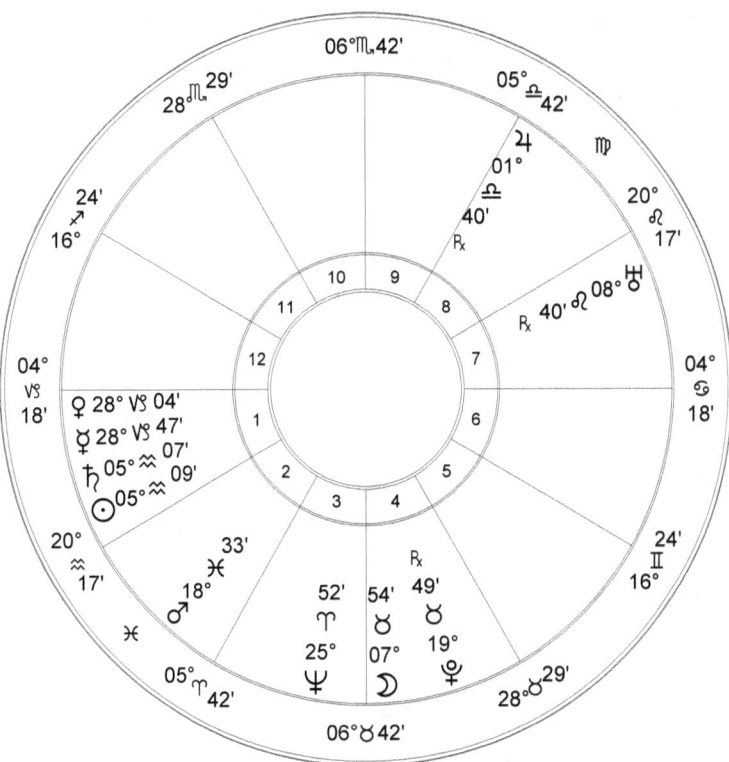

W. Somerset Maugham
January 25, 1874

be found sliding down into a valley of desperation. Whichever their orientation, it is as easy for them to change their course as it is to change the course of a steam engine once it has gathered momentum.

Fixed signs will generally be found to be set in their ways, busily applying themselves to their chosen occupation, with little or no interest in change or variation unless such a change would measurably improve their current situation. "This is what I do, and I like it this way. Why should I change? Why reinvent the wheel? If it ain't broke, don't fix it!" If a certain brand of shoe fits well and is comfortable and durable, they will buy these shoes until the company stops producing them. If a certain brand of coffee tastes better than any other, they will trudge ten miles through a raging blizzard to acquire it. Unless a change can be seen to somehow enhance the experience or improve productivity, the status quo is likely to be maintained. Change for its own sake or for the sake of action or excitement is not a common motivator for the fixed cross.

When reason and idealism take precedence over perception, as is the case in charts with a strong mutable and cardinal emphasis, the process of perception, although fundamental in nature, can be overlooked or even completely denied expression. When perceptions are denied recognition, inner conflict results. Common expressions of this conflict are: "I felt I should do this, but, well... it didn't seem to make sense," or, "I wanted to do the right thing, even if it didn't feel quite right." For the most part, at a very young age we are taught to think things through, to use reason and logic, and to consult books and experts to obtain the answers we need in life. "Use your head," we are told, and this is what we usually try to do, to the exclusion of one of our most important sources of information: our perceptions. The questions "What do you see? hear? taste? or feel?" would more appropriately favour the use of perceptions in evaluating life circumstances, and would prove to contribute a most beneficial

The Fixed Signs

aspect to the process if added to our educational protocol along with "What do you think?"

The beauty and at the same time the problem with perceptions is that they produce information that is personal and subjective in nature. Such a diversity of experience might, under certain circumstances, be considered problematic, especially in situations where standards and norms must be met. When twenty preschool children use a variety of colours to portray their perception of a pine tree, we are pleased to witness the expression of individual taste and experience, whereas if twenty factory employees are allowed to paint stop signs according to their own perceptions of the colour red, there will be problems with the consistency of the colour of the finished product. Clearly there is a time for perception and then there is a time for reason, but mostly, there is a time for a harmonious blending of both.

If a person's gut tells him that a certain course of action is right for him, in other words, if his perceived response is to pursue a certain direction, but his educated and trained mental processes tell him that he should "do the right thing," often requiring that he should ignore his feelings or natural inclinations and listen to his head or to the dictates of an external, wiser, and more authoritative source of information, an inner climate of disharmony is established. Fixed individuals who lack self-confidence, who have not been taught, and in many cases allowed, to trust and respect their perceptions and to make decisions that are in accordance with their inner selves, are likely to choose to listen to their head; that is, to "do the right thing" or to be reasonable.

The direction suggested by gut feelings might be perceived as leading to a solitary and sometimes frightening path, one for which these individuals have not been sufficiently prepared, one for which they may not feel equipped, a direction that may not elicit expressions of approval and support from others. In order to pursue their true path, however, fixed individuals must acquire sufficient self-confidence and a strong enough sense of self-worth to make the effort of fighting their solitary battle at least seem worthwhile. However, self-confidence and self-worth are usually the result of having pursued one's true path. Fixed individuals will often find themselves trapped in a vicious circle, where in order to obtain the confidence they seek, they must follow their heart, and to follow their heart, they must overcome their fears and insecurities.

"If only we could pull out our brain and use only our eyes."[1]
—Pablo Picasso

The fixed aspects of self-worth, enjoyment, and personal values have in the past generally not been encouraged and at times have been outright discouraged. Although differentness and uniqueness may be favourable attributes under certain circumstances, more often than not they are perceived as disruptive and difficult to manage, or as a threat to the status quo. Most people have encountered situations, either directly or indirectly, where someone has come up with a different way of doing things and was immediately confronted with a "don't rock the boat" response. It is much easier to manage a group of "sheep," or followers, than it is to steer a group of individualists.

Strong fixed-sign individuals will sometimes find themselves involuntarily marginalized, especially when they choose to follow their own set of values. Fixed signs evaluate life experiences primarily through perceptions. Social pressures, cultural influences, acquired values, and education will contribute to determining whether or not these individuals will be comfortable enough to trust these perceptions and eventually pursue their true path. A society that values duty, self-sacrifice, and respect for an established order may not be equipped to support the values of fixed individuals who choose a path for the simple reason that they like it.

---

1. Picasso was a Scorpio with six fixed planets, including the Ascendant and Ascendant ruler in fixed signs. It is interesting to note that he had a mutable Moon and so probably found himself pulled between perception and reason.

The Fixed Signs

At the turn of this new century, as many of us find ourselves more alienated than ever from the support of traditional religious teachings, we are introduced and are listening to the strong voices of authors such as Gary Zukav, Iyanla Vanzant, and Dr. Phil McGraw, who teach acceptance of self and listening to the "inner voice." Whereas in the past to consider "self" before "other" was seen as selfish, improper, or even wrongful behaviour, today people are spending millions of dollars on books, videos, and workshops that teach that you cannot be of any help to "others" if you haven't been able to help your "self." Oprah Winfrey, a great proponent of this revolution in self-awakening, and perhaps the single most important player in this growing tide given the scope of her popularity and influence in the media, is a native of the fixed sign Aquarius. With a total of six planets in the fixed signs, she no doubt speaks from personal experience when she advocates that we should take the time every day to "honour our spirit."

Fixed signs, at least at first glance, because of their constant and usually consistent flow of activity, seem to have "everything together," or "under control." They appear to have their lives sorted out, to be competent in what they are doing and know where they are going. This is in part because they tend to be focused on present events and circumstances, and in part because they tend to involve themselves in activities that reflect their competence, which contributes to the appearance of functionality under most circumstances, even during the most trying of times. They also choose activities that they like and with which they are familiar, increasing their level of stamina and self-confidence, which provide a high level of tolerance for stress and challenge. While cardinals are generally seeking to attain an ideal, and mutables are busy measuring up to a standard or model of reality, the fixed signs are trying, often unconsciously, to "be" or, more consciously in an externalized form, to express themselves in their dealings with the reality at hand. The fixed signs will take the idea or the plan initially generated by the cardinal cross and deploy all available talents and resources to make it a reality.

Astrological Crosses

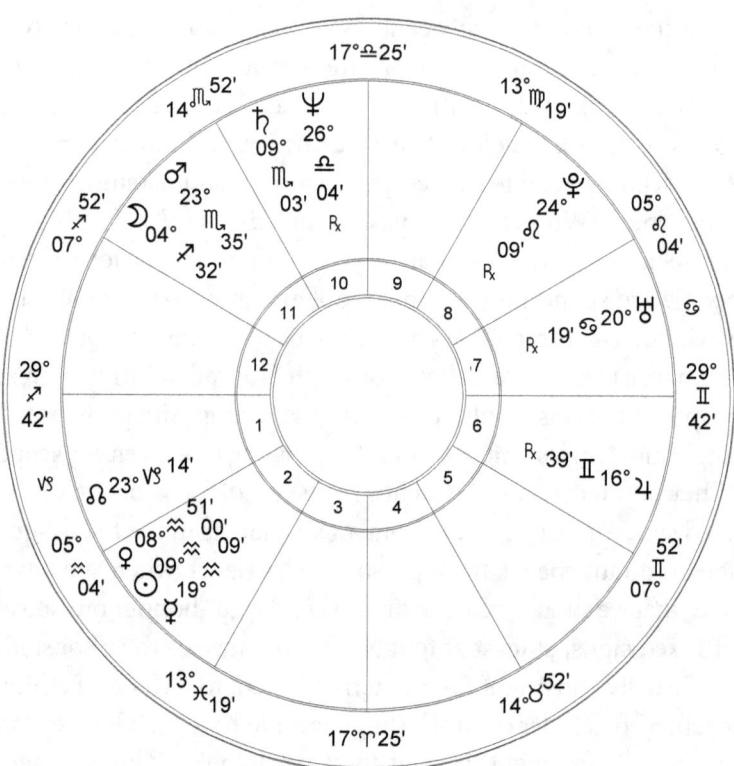

Oprah Winfrey
January 29, 1954

The Fixed Signs

The changes of season marked by the cardinal signs, and represented in the horoscope by the angular houses, are followed or succeeded, by mid season, represented by the fixed signs, or the succedent houses. The succedent houses are the houses of results, money, values (second house), shared resources, transformation, death (eighth house), love given, children, creations (fifth house), love received, friends, associates (eleventh house), and are naturally associated with the fixed signs Taurus, Leo, Scorpio, and Aquarius. An underlying current of value and worth weaves its way through these houses and through the fixed signs.

In *Astrology, How and Why it Works* Jones states that "The fixed sign people for the major part are absorbed in plans, projects, reasons, abstract evaluations and the general or over-all patterns of life. Consequently, they are the most difficult of the three groups to understand or describe. Their life is far more internal than in the other two cases. So much of their reaction is subjective that it frequently goes unnoticed, even by themselves at the moment. Their stand on everyday or practical matters is firm, and their presence in any situation is far from shrinking. Because their persistent struggle for self-evolution is not always recognized by others on normal contact, they may appear lazy or dull, and therefore uninteresting. When not analyzed in the light of the ideas they hold, they may seem extraordinarily stubborn in a superficial way, but are fundamentally open-minded because they are uninfluenced by other than their own judgments... Ultimately the most self-consistent of the three types, they are hardly ever understood, unless unusually articulate in some individual case."

It is interesting to note that Jones, although a native of the cardinal sign Libra, has a healthy dose of fixed planets, including a Moon-Saturn-Midheaven conjunction in Leo and a Mercury-Venus conjunction in Scorpio in the 12th house, no doubt contributing to his profound insights into this "most difficult of the three groups to describe," while his four mutable planets provide the "unusually articulate" ability to convey these perceptions.

The fixed signs can be seen as difficult to comprehend if one insists on measuring them against existing standards and conventions. In the first part of Jones' statement, the word *absorbed* is key to this definition of the fixed signs, and should be underlined. Fixed signs remain close to the product and to the result of an operation or project, and will not waste time on the "plan, the reasons and abstract evaluations" unless they are an integral part of the process of accomplishment, in which case they will willingly participate and even immerse themselves in these activities.

> "Beauty is an ecstasy; it is as simple as hunger. There is really nothing to be said about it. It is like the perfume of a rose: you can smell it and that is all."
>
> —W. Somerset Maugham

In Bériault's introduction to the crosses, he assigned the Ptolemaic aspect of Beauty to the fixed cross, a far more interesting and appealing designation than the traditional attributes of "steady but dull." At first glance, I was relieved to discover that I belonged to such a distinguished group, a group that had suddenly risen from the ashes of a long-standing lackluster reputation and blossomed into something with appeal and desirability. But not all fixed-sign individuals are beautiful, I pondered, so what does beauty mean in terms of the fixed cross?

The essence of beauty lies in the fact that a thing or person is beautiful by the simple virtue of its existence. In less abstract terms, a thing is what it is, and that's what gives it value. We are all familiar with the expression "Beauty is in the eye of the beholder," and, in truth, beauty is very much a result of the process of perception. If we take the time to experience the essence of a thing or a person, to truly know this thing or person, then we will experience its beauty. If we take the time to listen and get to know an individual, eventually we will discover the inherent beauty that lies in the process of individual emergence that is manifesting deep within the soul. Each person harbours such a potential unfolding, in some cases (especially the strong fixed

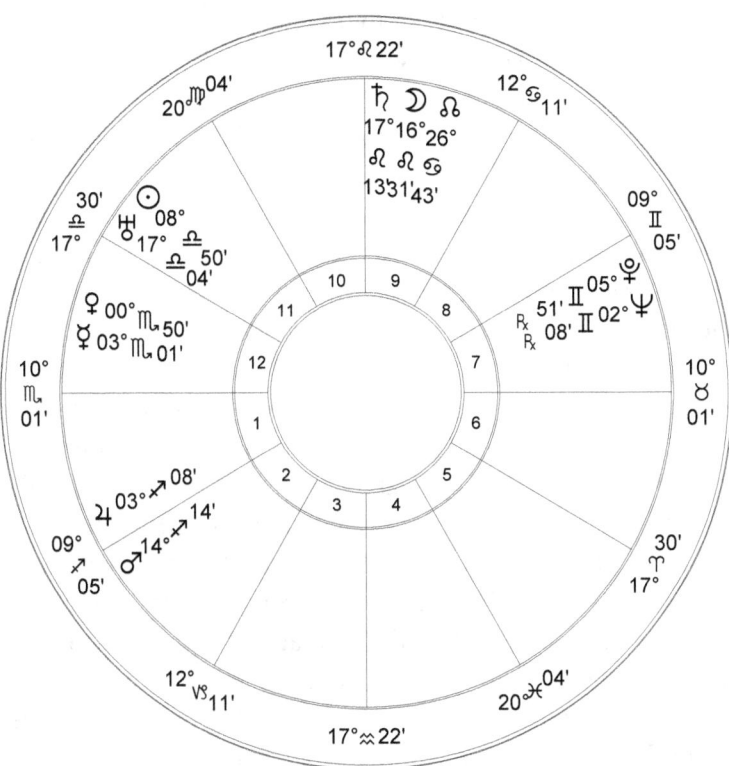

Marc Edmund Jones
October 1, 1888

signs) it is more evident than in others. Look to the fixed placements of your own chart to see the beauty of the individual that lies within your soul.

Several years ago, in the middle of March, I had spent the morning cleaning the house and the afternoon giving the car its first wash since the previous summer. It was still too cold to stand outside with the hose, and so my dear Taurus father had warmed up his garage for me. The Moon, ruler of my sixth house of daily chores, was transiting my first house. I missed most of the sunshine that day, but many people thoroughly enjoyed this first mild and sunny Saturday, a welcome prelude to the new season that was inching its way toward us. When you live at 45° north and 72° west, you take the fair weather very seriously. Later that day, a fixed-sign friend and I drove out for dinner with some former coworkers. It was dark already, but the day had clearly made an impact on my passenger. She'd been through a very difficult spell the previous couple of months, and all the while had to maintain job, family and home. We chatted about different things, but what stood out for me was her interpretation of the day. "It felt so good," she said, "what with the day being longer and the light coming from a different angle, it's always different when spring approaches." In her experience, it had been a beautiful day, and that experience had momentarily allowed her to escape the challenges of her life. The fixed evaluation of the day was based on a sensory appreciation—longer days, more light, and the promise of the beauty of spring. A mutable person might have pointed out that it had been a good day, but not as warm as had been forecast, and a cardinal might have described at length where he went, what he did, all wrapped up in the excitement of the movement.

Let's recall the quotation from the third interview in the FCA newsletter, "Directions": "We go through this conference experience, I think, for the sheer beauty of the experience." It may now be quite evident which cross was speaking; in fact, the author of these words is a native of the fixed sign Leo. It was a simple response and one which spoke from the heart of the person's experience, and was indeed so very fixed.

The Voice of Desire

To the fixed sign, the fundamental driving force is *desire*. It is virtually impossible to reason with fixed-sign individuals who have made up their mind about something, especially if the decision is based on the fact that they "like" the thing in question. This may appear as unreasonable, irresponsible, or childish behaviour to the non-fixed person, and might, under certain circumstances, be perceived as behaviour that smacks of outright disobedience to authority or disrespect for the norms or rules, and sometimes it is just that. Yet, this does not mean that fixed-sign individuals have no respect for the law, that they never grow up and assume responsibilities, or that they will never play by the rules. Nor does it mean that fixed-sign natives have no inner motive or reason or no set goals in life. Fixed signs are, in fact, more concerned with the actual satisfaction of a desire, or the immediate application of a skill or knowledge, than with planning for an intangible goal or with the justification of their actions to the satisfaction of some external standard.

It is in the nature of the desire, in its intrinsic value, that we find the reason for the fixed sign's motivation and subsequent actions. The fixed cross is the cross of values, on all levels. In particular, it is the cross of inner value, of self-validation and of self-worth. Where fixed placements are found in the chart, whether house cusps or planetary positions, is not only where you will find that which is of value and that which is important in life, but also where you will find opportunities to develop a sense of self-worth. This is where you will find a special talent or an ability of great value, one that can, given the appropriate care and attention, be developed and used for your benefit and perhaps for profit.

Look for a fixed house cusp for an area of activity that will provide the means to distinguish yourself in a unique and individualistic way. A fixed third house, for example, might indicate an ability to write, while a fixed eleventh house might indicate a talent, whether latent or expressed, for understanding and creating social policy. Whatever the talent, it is likely to have a very personal and even private feel to it and is likely to be expressed from the heart. If developed and used in the course of a lifetime, such talents can impart a deep sense of personal satisfaction.

Each of us has the twelve signs in our natal chart, and the importance of certain values over others will be determined by planetary distribution among these signs. Even if an individual does not have any planets in the fixed signs, it does not mean that he or she does not have a sense of self worth or is lacking in a set of personal values. It just means that value and self-worth may be components of lesser importance in the life process of those who have little fixed energy. Basically, fixed-sign individuals are driven to accomplish goals that fulfill their desires and that reflect their inner value structure. In short, they must "like" what they do, or at least they aspire to do what they like. Look to your fixed placements to find the areas of life that will bring true pleasure into your life.

While watching the television show *Entertainment Tonight* with my daughter one evening, a young actor was interviewed about an encounter he'd recently had with the law. Okay, so I watch *E.T.* now and then, well, perhaps often. With a fifth-house ruler conjunct the Sun in Leo, I have a legitimate excuse for enjoying entertainment gossip! As the young man was saying into the camera, "We have to enjoy our work. We're entitled to enjoy what we're doing." I immediately picked up on the fixed intonation of his words and exclaimed, "That's so fixed!" At which point my daughter looked up nonchalantly and replied, "Of course, that's Christian Slater. He's a Leo." By the language he used, he expressed how the value of the experience, more specifically the *personal* value, is fundamental to the motivations of the fixed-cross individual. Just try to convince your Taurus or Aquarius buddy to sign up for an activity for which he has absolutely no interest or liking. No amount of argument on the side of duty and obligation or in the name of friendship will get him to move in the direction you are suggesting if he has no inclination to go there, even if he is the most open-minded Aquarian. Irresponsible or unreasonable, you might say? It might seem so to those who are guided by reason or duty (mutables), or by ideals or a need for excitement (cardinals). Perhaps it is just that the fixed signs really know what they like.

What me, stubborn? The fixed signs have traditionally been characterized as being steady, fixed, steadfast, and stubborn, which, for the most part, is true. However, observation has proven that stubbornness does not belong to the fixed signs alone. It would appear that each cross, and for that matter each sign, has its own unique brand of stubbornness. The intransigence expressed when mutable signs decide to sink their heels into a chosen position, usually backed by logical and faultless rationalization, will readily be perceived as impossible stubbornness by anyone trying to influence or change their position. Cardinals, on the other hand, will feel supported by the strength of their convictions. It is impossible to convince cardinals to act against their religious or political beliefs, or their principles. They may decide to change these beliefs over their life span, but this will be a choice of their own, or may be predicated by a representative of authority whom they hold in high regard.

What makes the stubbornness of the fixed sign seem more rigid than that of the other two crosses is that it is usually born of an internal motivation and is thus not easily defended with the use of logic or reason. "I want to study dance because this is what interests me and this is what I like. It doesn't matter that there may be little chance of obtaining a job in my chosen field; I'd rather dance and be poor than to not try at all." These words were spoken by my older Taurus daughter just before starting a contemporary dance program at university. Also, the measure of satisfaction for the fixed signs is largely internal rather than external; for example, "I'm doing this because I like it," rather than, "I'm doing this because it will help move my career forward" (cardinal), or, "I'm doing this because it is the right thing to do, or this is what I should be doing" (mutable). Again, the stubbornness of the fixed sign can appear illogical, pointless or even self-indulgent as viewed from the outside, but it may be the force which keeps these individuals from deviating from their true path.

Productivity, Validation, and Personal Satisfaction

According to deVore in his *Encyclopedia of Astrology*, the "Fixed or Grave signs or Executive types . . . are the powerhouses of the zodiac—reservoirs of energy; . . . the builders of the world. The fixed sign tenacity is depended upon to support or stabilize the leading (cardinal) signs." Indeed, the fixed signs are the workhorses of the zodiac, and in positions of authority they can be taskmasters. They are not fond of people who do not take their job seriously and who do not put out his best. Fixed-sign individuals are happiest and at their most productive when they are doing what they enjoy doing, which is why they usually seek out employment that provides at least some degree of enjoyment or personal satisfaction.

Fixed-sign natives are the doers of the zodiac, and will usually be found in the process of actualizing something, whether big or small, anything at all as long as there is some semblance of accomplishment in the process. They have a fundamental need to be engaged in some type of meaningful activity, the "meaningful" nature of the activity naturally being defined by the value set of the individual. Henry Ford, a native of the fixed sign Leo, and an interesting case in point, has long been considered the founder of modern automobile mass production, while English engineer and inventor Richard Trevithick, a cardinal-sign individual,

The Fixed Signs

is credited with the invention of the steam engine. Here we have an illustration of the difference in focus between the fixed sign, which is focused on production, and the cardinal sign, which is focused on developing an idea.

At a young age, Ford indulged his natural curiosity for the workings of machinery by tinkering with farming equipment. This fascination eventually led to a machinist apprenticeship in Detroit where he encountered steam and internal combustion engines. As a Leo native, wanting to do things himself, he set out to develop his own engine, which he placed in a four-wheel carriage. His goal was to produce an affordable car that would replace the horse and buggy and railroad as chief means of transportation. He achieved this goal with the Model T, because of the production methods he used. To keep costs down, he bought factories and made his own parts, and bought his own steel mills and iron mines as well as his own railroads and ship lines to transport his materials and products. He used an efficient assembly line system, paid workers on a daily wage basis, and revolutionized the manufacturing process.

Ford's chart shows four fixed and four cardinal planets, combining cardinal vision and ideas with fixed hard work, persistence, and productivity, a combination often found in the charts of entrepreneurs and business leaders. A cardinal placement for Saturn is quite common in the charts of builders and engineers, especially in Libra, Aries, and Capricorn. As a fixed sign, Ford no doubt enjoyed his research and his work, and his high level of energy (cardinal) and passion for his interests (fixed) contributed to a long and productive life. Note also that one of his main concerns was to develop an affordable vehicle that everyone could own, with the issue of value often being of importance to the fixed-sign native. In effect, Ford brought together all the resources that he needed and focused on the production process to deliver a product that everyone would desire. Desire leads to purchases, and purchases lead to profits, an effective motivational factor for a fixed-sign native.

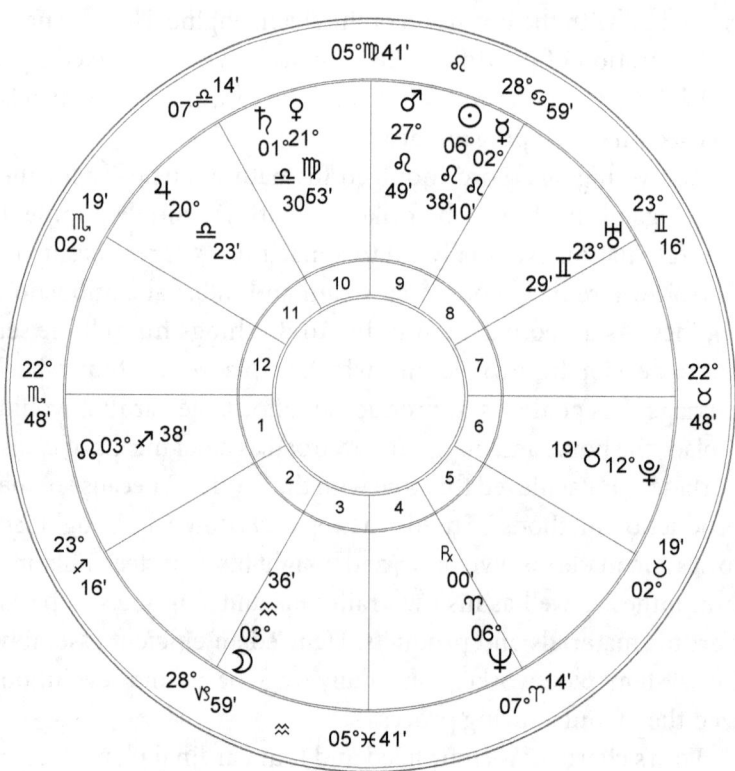

Henry Ford
July 30, 1863

The Fixed Signs

During a lecture on personal success that I gave at a business women's dinner (a group of non astrologers), I pointed out the basic qualities and attributes of each of the crosses and how these might apply to them in the exercise of their professions. I described how the Cardinals are the visionaries, the motivators who like to plan and start projects and get things moving and shaking, while the mutables are the relators, and are talented at networking and establishing contacts with clients and colleagues, at distributing goods and services. The fixed signs, I explained, are the doers, and are more comfortable at their work stations or in their offices doing the work they value and like rather than networking or talking about it. Just then, a young woman whom I had already suspected of being a Scorpio native, a self-employed personal trainer whose services I employed, quickly raised her hand and cried, "That's not true, I'm a Scorpio, and I'm here!" I smiled but did not argue the point, knowing full well that although we sat at round tables covered in crisp white linen table cloths eating fine French cuisine, this was a net-*work*-ing dinner, and that she would more than likely be home with her husband and young children if this were anything but work-related.

At the following meeting, at my trainer's suggestion, I brought along my workout sheets. I had some questions concerning the routine she had designed for me, and so I discretely handed her the papers during a convenient break in the meeting. She promptly began to redesign the problematic segment of my workout. Several minutes later, she returned the sheets with new exercises clearly described and drawn up in little stick figures. Grateful for her thoroughness and prompt attention, yet somewhat ill at ease for having imposed on her during the dinner, I thanked her and responded to her queries, indicating that I understood her notes. Feeling a little guilty for having "made her work" so much during the meeting, as unobtrusively as possible I crept back to my table with my workout tucked discretely underneath my arm.

When the meeting was finished, I found her sitting at another table, busily giving explanations to another client. She had just finished redesigning another woman's workout. "There you go," I teased. "Remember what I said at the last meeting about the fixed signs? You're busy at work!" Feeling as though she must defend her position, she added, "But I like to get results." To which I replied, "Exactly my point." Fixed signs like to be doing their thing, whatever it may be, and as a Scorpio, she naturally feels that it is important to "get results," the transforming, improving side of the sign. It is not uncommon to find the fixed signs married to their occupations, with Aquarians being the most guilty of this trait.

Odile operates an office services and translation business from her home. I had known Odile for a little over a year, and noted that she had managed to find herself in the position of secretary for two of the business networking groups to which I belonged. She worked quietly and with the utmost discretion, always maintained a positive and friendly disposition, had an above-average mastery of word processing and other software tools, and had, as I discovered when we started to pass email jokes back and forth, an earthy and gritty sense of humour. I suspected a Scorpio and Taurus influence in the chart. On one occasion, when someone offered to relieve her of her reception duties at the door during a business meeting, she quickly and firmly assured us that she much preferred to work the table (collecting membership fees and keeping track of attendance) than to schmooze and network with the others. As always, Odile did her advertising by showing what she could do. She clearly enjoys her work and would rather work than socialize—a definite fixed-sign indicator.

Her established facility for learning and using software and technology suggested an Aquarian influence, a fact which I had overlooked but was quick to recognize when someone mentioned that her birthday was coming up and I realized she was, in fact, a native of that sign. I was still convinced of a Scorpio and Taurus influence, and so I dared ask for her birth date, which revealed five fixed planets including a Scorpio Moon. Not wanting to overstep the bounds of common courtesy (I highly respect

The Fixed Signs

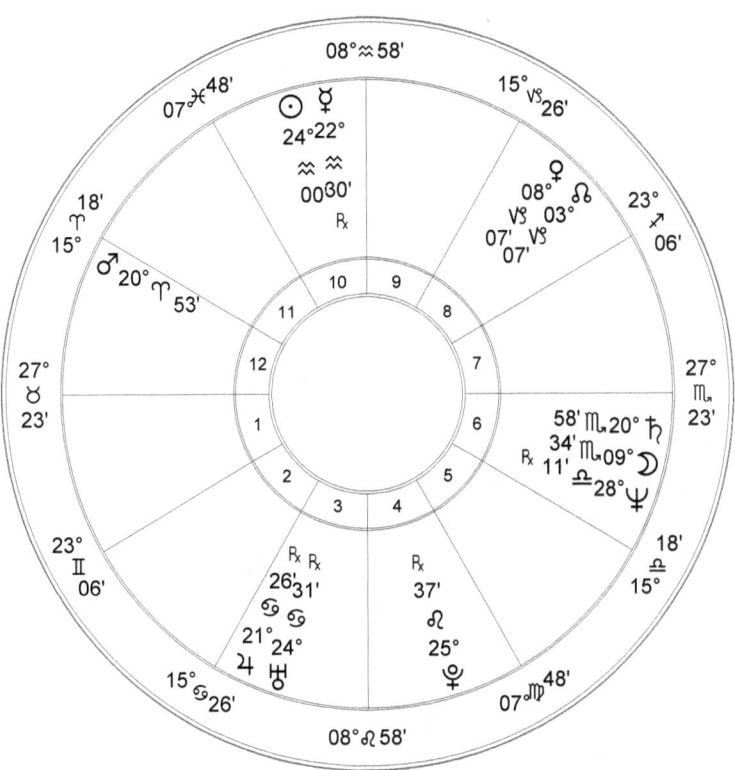

Odile

a person's privacy), yet unable to settle for not having found the Taurus influence, I let curiosity get the better of me and fired off an email asking if she knew her time of birth. (For some strange reason, I felt safer behind the anonymity of the electronic postal system). Lo and behold, there it was in her response, an "around noon" birth time, giving a strong likelihood of Taurus rising.

Fixed signs can have difficulty with facsimiles of reality; they need the real thing in their hands. It is difficult for them to theorize, symbolize, or even make caricatures of reality, at least until they have made the conscious realization that this is what they are doing. At the same time, fixed signs do not readily learn from theory, illustration, or symbolism, or even analogy, unless the latter is very explicit. They need to get their hands dirty, to be immersed in the experience, to have firsthand knowledge of a situation in order for it to be a part of their reality. What they create, in their minds, is the real thing. Some time ago I asked my brother Michael, an accomplished composer, if he could make a wave file for my computer using the theme from the television show *The X-Files*. I fully expected that this would be an extremely simple task for him as he had just hummed the opening bars as a comical emphasis to something we had been discussing. His reply was, "Oh, not just like that. I'll need to hear the original on tape first." I argued, "Oh, come on, you just hummed it a minute ago, it's easy for you to do." To which he replied, "I need to hear the original to get all the instruments right, you know how I am a perfectionist." In his fixed mind (nine fixed planets), he saw only that he needed the actual music from which he could make an exact copy. There was no room for improvisation or experimentation, abilities that are more readily found with a mutable-sign influence.

I mentioned to a mutable friend that a Laura Secord outlet had just opened at the mall, where they sold chocolate at a fraction of the usual cost. I had remained stuck on the fact that the chocolates were piled into large five-pound plain cardboard boxes, packaging that was not terribly elegant for gift giving (as you may have guessed, the fixed cross is my strong suite). My friend with a mutable Sun, Mercury, and Venus immediately responded with, "But you just have to put them into other containers, maybe a cute cup or something." I wanted to kick myself for not having seen the obvious. She took a situation, unsightly packaging, and instantly connected it to many possibilities, a wide range of containers, hence making the yummy treats presentable as gifts. Voilà! Of course, if I had really desired to offer the chocolates as gifts, my willfulness (fixed) would eventually have led me to study the problem and find solutions, perhaps look for another box into which I could slip the large box, or maybe consider wrapping the box. Notice how fixed signs will attempt to work with what is there, even if it doesn't work! After several attempts at trying to fix the problem, I might then have considered changing containers, at which point I would have found myself to be wickedly clever. Any mutable sign would simply think that I was not terribly imaginative, and at that moment, I wasn't. Fortunately for creative fixed-sign native Martha Stewart, she has four mutable planets to help her bend wicker into any shape she can imagine.

Identity and Creativity

> "The reasonable man adapts himself to the conditions that surround him . . . The unreasonable man adapts surrounding conditions to himself . . . All progress depends on the unreasonable man"[2]
>
> —George Bernard Shaw

While being aware of the external events at hand, fixed-sign individuals are also deeply aware of the inner self. The fact that *I am doing an action, and producing a result* is as important as the product, or result of the action. With the fixed signs, there is a strong identification of the doer with the action being done

---

2. Shaw had five fixed planets, including the Sun in Leo and the Moon in Taurus, plus a fixed Midheaven.

or with the object of their creative efforts. As fixed signs identify with their creation, if this creation is rejected or criticized, the self feels rejected or criticized. This is especially the case if the sense of self is young, vulnerable, or in some way weak. As much as they take great pride in showing their works to others, fixed-sign artists might hold on to their works far longer than is necessary due to this inner vulnerability.

When lacking the confidence to follow their heart or when circumstances are not propitious, fixed individuals can convince themselves to take a path that does not reflect their inner values. In such cases, they tend to underperform. Fixed-sign individuals who have a healthy sense of confidence in themselves and in their abilities will often be found to walk to the beat of their own drum. Sometimes they appear to be in a world unto themselves, and in a way they are, for they are driven from within, rather than from without. Following a path of their own design may cause fixed-sign individuals to not quite fit into the established patterns and moulds, the proverbial square pegs that don't quite fit into the round holes.

When fixed signs take on a hobby, and if they enjoy what they are doing, they can just about turn their hobby into a manufacturing process, and some of them actually do, Martha Stewart being a prime example of this phenomenon. Some time ago, I had the pleasure of being initiated into the art of home wine-making by my Aquarian friend Betty; her chart has a total of six fixed planets plus a fixed Ascendant. Betty had begun wine-making a few years before and had taken such a liking to it that she eventually volunteered to make wine for some of her friends. On the day I went to start my first batch, she had seven carboys lined up in a row on her dining room floor! Clearly, Betty enjoys making wine.

Besides spending her workdays sorting through a multitude of translation and documentation-related challenges, my friend Odile is also an accomplished amateur gardener. Her outdoor home garden, as well as her indoor experiments with anything from rose grafts to imported wildflowers, have won her the

The Fixed Signs

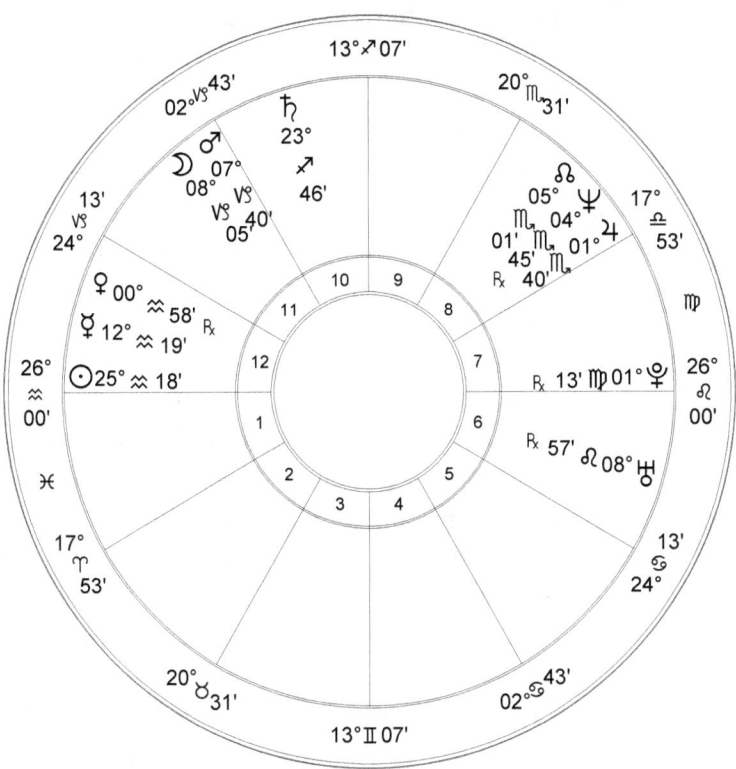

Betty

acclaim of local garden enthusiasts. If it has a seed, Odile can make it bloom. A hobby is an excellent avenue of self-expression for all fixed-sign individuals, especially for those who have difficulty releasing their creative energies.

The important thing to consider when evaluating the chart of a fixed-sign individual, especially the creative types, is the "what" of the person's occupation. Is the person doing something that is simple, enjoyable, or perhaps easy, just to pass the time because it is in his nature to do something? Or is the person doing something that will provide sufficient challenge to allow him to grow into his full potential? When faced with a temporary block in the creative process, the fixed signs can turn to the next favourite line of activity. It is rare for a fixed-sign person to have "nothing to do." For example, Michael, the composer, will readily abandon his computer to spend a day creating a gourmet meal for friends, an activity at which he excels. When I can no longer write, I will turn to my other favourite activities, such as gardening, baking, or some home renovation project (believe me, I have many alternatives to writing!). Betty's main creative abilities are not limited to wine-making. She is also a very gifted painter; the wine-making is a secondary source of enjoyment.

As an interesting addendum, while revising the manuscript for this new edition of *The Crosses*, I had the opportunity to work with Betty at a Christmas fundraiser for the benefit of families of sick children. Not surprisingly, Betty had attracted to herself the huge task of recruiting volunteers and organizing schedules for the holiday rush. True to her fixed-sign nature, when the volunteers found themselves experiencing a break in the activity of wrapping, she asked if they wouldn't mind preparing gift boxes in advance of Christmas Eve, the biggest day for the organization. And so it was that the long tables were turned into busy production lines, with eager volunteers turning out all manner of creative designs for the gift boxes.

I have noticed that any type of productive activity will provide satisfaction when the fixed person's creative juices have become

The Fixed Signs

blocked. There can be pitfalls in this shift from one creative activity to another in that it occurs so naturally. Before long, the more-challenging creative activity, painting, writing, composing, has been entirely supplanted by other activities that are usually less significant, perhaps practical, or even necessary on some level, such as cleaning out the garage or painting a room, but definitely not in the same league as the original creative activity. It's easier to cook a gourmet meal than to compose an opera, to design a rose garden than to write a book, to experiment with a batch of Bordeaux than to complete an original painting, or perhaps to fix a leaky faucet than to come up with a new website design. The true creative activities, expressions of the deeper inner self, can too easily be allowed to slip behind the day job or the more mundane activities of everyday life. The creative process is a fragile thing, indeed, and should be treated with the delicacy and nurturing it requires so that it may flourish and grow into the full expression of the inner beauty of the artist.

An added challenge for creative fixed people is that they tend to identify with the object of their creative process: "I *am* the music, the painting, or the book. This quilt, this music, or this painting is a part of me, I cannot let it go until it really reflects what I want to say." They will work on their creation over and over again, perfecting it, developing it, holding on to it, very often fearful of releasing it into a world that may not welcome or accept it with the appreciation, understanding, and love it deserves. When the music is played, when the painting is seen, when the book is read, "others will know me," and this level of vulnerability can be a very frightening prospect.

Watch for transits and progressions through the fixed signs for the urge to develop creative abilities. To explore your creativity does not mean that you should quit your day job and take up a paint brush; creativity can manifest in many areas of activity. Creative self-expression requires only that you allow your inner self to find a voice, to direct your actions in a way that reveals something about who you are and how you perceive the world.

Growing up Fixed

Unlike mutable children, who will find a way of communicating their needs, or cardinal children, who can push themselves onto their environment or somehow make their presence known, fixed children are much more the loner type. Their parents will have the impression that all is well, that their child's needs are satisfied. But fixed children need not only to be told and shown that they are loved, but also that they are worthy of this love. Empty words or mechanical gestures of affection will quickly be detected. The words must convey true feelings of affection and should not only be expressed as terms of endearment, which is the case with all children, but is even more important with the fixed ones. For example, "sweetie," "honey," or "dear" should be expressed with real feeling, and not as habitual replacements for the child's real name.

A strong sense of self is essential to the healthy development of fixed children, and in cultures where self-denial and self-effacement are taught and encouraged, much anguish and inner suffering can result for the strong fixed-sign children. In this sense, the fixed aspects of the zodiac refer to that which is "selfish" in an individual. As the perceptual experience of reality is subjective, the importance of adequate self-validation cannot be stressed enough. These children need to be encouraged to trust their perceptions and to express themselves in their own manner and style. It is okay for these children to focus on themselves in their youth; in fact, it is essential that they develop a strong sense of self so that they can grow up and feel secure enough to give of themselves without the fear of loss.

Being fixed and very one-pointed, fixed signs have fewer options for experimenting with various types of behaviour. If what they are is not acceptable, then nothing is acceptable; this can lead to a path of depression and despair and ultimately even to self-destructive behaviour. On the other hand, if fixed children are encouraged to be who they really are, they will be very

The Fixed Signs

autonomous, self-motivated, and capable of embarking on long hard paths of self-discipline and training that other children might not be able to endure. Their autonomy must not be mistaken for lack of need of support from others. It is just that they do not consider seeking help outside themselves.

This ease with "doing" begins early in life. A mother once told me of a fright she had experienced when nowhere in the house could she locate her four-year-old daughter (five fixed planets and a fixed Ascendant). She had described her little girl as always busy playing with her toys, quietly, for hours on end. She found her that day asleep in her toy box; undoubtedly tired after a long day of play, she had curled up and fallen asleep. At Christmas time one year, with family members chatting over wine and hors d'oeuvres while the holiday dinner was being made ready, my eight-year-old Scorpio niece (four fixed planets plus a fixed Midheaven and Ascendant) took out her candlemaking kit, moved her play table into the center of the action, that is, in the entranceway between the kitchen and dining room, and proceeded to quietly and contentedly create little wax candles to set on the tables for the event. She was content to be engaged in a creative activity, on her own, while the chattering of family and friends continued around her. Although the resulting works of art, small and fragile of construction, received but passing praise as the group moved on to the meal being served, our pint-sized artist remained poised and satisfied with her efforts. Clearly her need for creative self-expression far outweighed her need for interaction (only two mutable planets) or for praise. Fixed children try to communicate by their works, by their drawings, and with their bodies.

4

The Mutable Cross

Gemini, Virgo, Sagittarius, Pisces

"There is no pleasure to me without communication: there is not so much as a sprightly thought comes into my mind that it does not grieve me to have produced alone, and that I have no one to tell it to."[1]

—Michel de Montaigne

The Power of Two

When I first began to study astrology (what seems like a lifetime ago now), there were very few books available on the subject in our local occult bookstore, the New Age not having yet been born. So it was that my very first astrology book was a hardcover edition of Margaret Hone's excellent book *The Modern Textbook of Astrology*. I was young at the time, certainly naive about life and the world and perhaps a little bit green for studies in astrology, since, as I later learned, a certain degree of maturity

---

1. French essayist. Sun and Neptune in Pisces, Ascendant in Gemini.

and life experience is essential to fostering an understanding of human nature, an important ingredient in astrological interpretation. Nevertheless, proud of my find, and so eager to learn, I began to study my first official textbook. When I reached the section describing the quadruplicities (or qualities), I was disappointed to read that the fixed signs "... will not be so good at getting things going, but will guard and conserve that which is started ... Their faults may be those of inertia, of lack of imagination, a lack of quick adaptability to circumstances." However, on reading the description of the mutable signs, I was a bit relieved to have been born fixed, apparently the lesser of two evils: "These signs [mutable signs] are also called the 'Common' signs. The common people are the people in general, hence the word has come to mean those who are usual or ordinary and those who serve." The description is qualified with the following statement: "From this it must not be gathered that there are no distinguished people in whose maps mutability predominates. Nevertheless, there is a *desire to serve* in many of these." The lack of mutables in my own chart no doubt spoke of my youthful lack of fondness for the idea of servitude; interestingly enough, however, I ended up in a profession in a service industry. Perhaps there is some truth to the idea that we seek that which we lack.

For the most part, the mutable signs have traditionally been described as changeable, uncertain, versatile, unstable, and easily influenced, traits that can be found in these signs, but, by far, are not the only characteristics of this complex cross. Mutables have the ability to experiment with multiple facets as well as multiple versions of reality; they are not tied to their perceptions, as are the fixed signs, or to their principles and ideals, as are the cardinal signs. What some perceive as inconstancy or unreliability in the mutable signs are, in fact, versatility and flexibility.

Although the power of this cross works in a more subtle and sometimes insidious manner than does the seemingly more overt power of the fixed and cardinal crosses, it should not be underestimated. Just because mutables are not drawn to power, as are the cardinals, it does not mean that they are not sensitive to it or aware of it. Mutables simply do not play the game as overtly and with as much fanfare as do the others. They are much more subtle and even devious in their approach, claiming power by establishing a position that provides them with the ability to control and manipulate people and circumstances according to their own designs. This type of power often goes unrecognized by the two other crosses, who may not possess such a subtle manner and style.

> *"I know I have the body of a weak and feeble woman, but I have the heart and stomach of a king, and of a king of England too."*[2]
>
> —Queen Elizabeth I

This quotation from a speech given by Queen Elizabeth I, a native of the mutable sign Virgo with four mutable planets, is indicative of a strong, determined, and courageous character, traits that served her well throughout the span of her life. This mutable energy, combined with an equal dose of cardinal energy, provided Elizabeth with the ambition, drive, and clarity of purpose that she needed to successfully manage the social, economic, religious, and political challenges of a turbulent time. She effectively ruled for nearly a half century, a period regarded as the most glorious in England's history. Although the mutable signs can be "changeable, uncertain, versatile, unstable, and easily influenced," they do also possess essential characteristics that allow them to acquire and wield power in their own unique way.

> *"She made it plain to her advisers that she, not they, would steer the ship of state, declaring: 'I will have here but one mistress and no master.'"*
>
> —Queen Elizabeth I

---

2. Elizabeth I (1533-1603). Excerpt from a speech given August 8, 1588, to troops at Tilbury, England, on the approach of the Spanish Armada.

Astrological Crosses

Elizabeth acquired an excellent education in her youth at the hands of a distinguished Cambridge scholar. Revealing a particular gift for languages, she became fluent in Latin, Greek, Italian, and French. One of Elizabeth's strong points was her natural mutable intelligence, which she used to establish ties and create an entourage of experts on whom she could call for advice during the course of the administration of her duties. Yet although she had access to some of the brightest minds to help her make her decisions, she would not allow anyone to control her own mind.

"I am your anointed Queen. I will never be by violence constrained to do anything. I thank God I am endued with such qualities that if I were turned out of the Realm in my petticoat I were able to live in any place in Christendom."
—Queen Elizabeth I

Under normal circumstances, the mutable signs do not seek glory and power for their own sake, as the cardinal signs might do, nor do they seek power as a means to an end, as the fixed signs might do. For the mutable signs, power and glory come more as a consequence of a series of actions, choices, and opportunities, which is possibly the reason why there are fewer stories about prominent mutable persons throughout history than there are about cardinal-sign persons. Naturally this in no way implies that the mutable signs are less capable than the other signs, only that they are less inclined to seek the visibility and acclamation associated with worldly success.

One of the principle strengths of the mutable signs stems from their ability to deal with circumstances and people through a process of association or relation. In any given situation, each cross will respond to and interpret reality in its own unique manner. The cardinal cross will respond to "the impact" of a situation: "This touches me, this makes me feel happy, sad, elated, excited." The fixed cross will respond through identification with itself or through personal experience: "This is like me, I know this," or, "I like this, I dislike this." The mutable cross individual will respond

The Mutable Cross

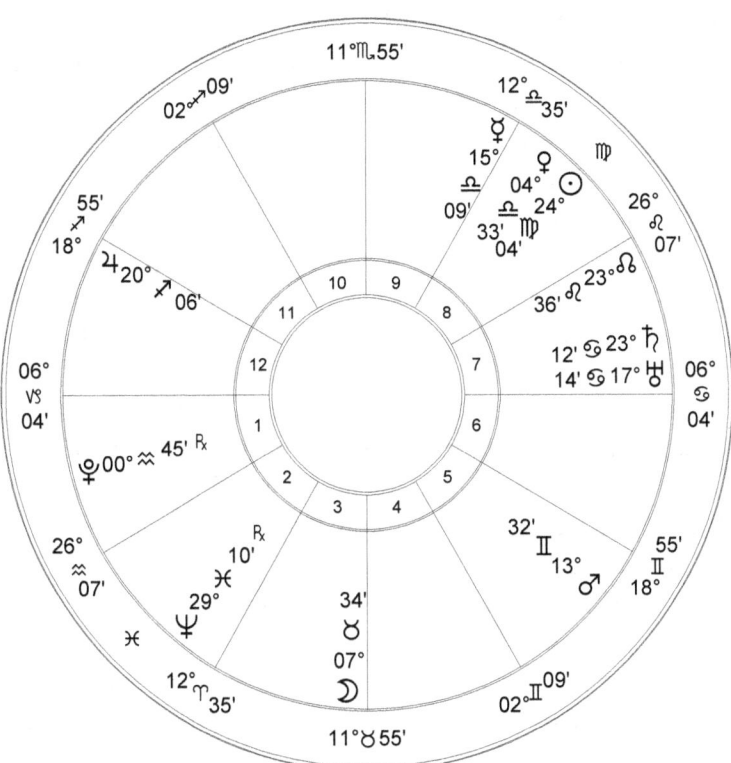

Queen Elizabeth I
September 7, 1533

by immediately making associations: "I saw this in a book, this is common knowledge, so-and-so experienced the same circumstances"; then, depending on the individual's motives, needs, or desires at the time, the mutable person will process the information and classify it for immediate or later use.

Mutable signs can be very quick at processing information, even trivial information; consequently, the learning aspect of the experience may occur much more quickly for mutables than for cardinal or fixed-sign individuals. They can be very quick-witted and versatile, they tend to be skilled at the art of repartee, and some make excellent stand-up comics such as Pisces Billy Crystal, Sagittarius Rich Little, and Gemini Bob Hope. They are usually articulate and quite capable at handling the most complex arts of protocol, and have good communication skills. This ability to establish relationships quickly under a variety of circumstances endows the mutable signs with an important advantage in many social situations.

To the mutable-sign individual, most life situations are experienced *in relationship* to something or someone that is external to them; hence, is born the dualistic nature of the signs. DeVore describes the mutable signs as "representing the arc in which there is a perpetual condition of slowing down in readiness to turn a corner; a mobilisation for action, and the indecision which results or accompanies it; were symbolized by concepts which would express this duality—the twins (Gemini), the two deep-water sea-horses (Pisces), or the half-man, half-horse of the Archer (Sagittarius); hence also called the Dual or the Double-bodied Signs; and by some, the Common or Flexed Signs. They are the minds of their Triplicity, with their quickness and versatility acting as mediators between the Leading and the Fixed Signs. They have been called the 'reconcilers of the universe.'" In this passage, we get a clear sense of the mutable-sign relationship with the cadent houses of the horoscope (third, sixth, ninth, and twelfth), which are defined as the houses of human relationships and the houses of transition, as they provide the link between the quadrants of the horoscope wheel

The Voice of Reason

> "Reason sits firm and holds the reins, and she will not let the feelings burst away and hurry her to wild chasms. The passions may rage furiously, like true heathens, as they are; and the desires may imagine all sorts of vain things: but judgement shall still have the last word in every argument, and the casting vote in every decision."
>
> —Charlotte Brontë

Ms. Brontë was a native of the fixed sign Taurus, but had four planets plus the Midheaven and Ascendant in mutable signs. This passage hints at a likely inner struggle between an intense and very present desire nature, as indicated by Sun in Taurus opposed Jupiter in Scorpio, and a strong need to conform to the dictates of reason and rationality, with Mars square Pluto in mutable signs and the Midheaven and Ascendant in mutable Gemini and Virgo, the intensity of this struggle being given added fuel due to the nature of the planets involved (Mars and Pluto).

The application of mental energy for the purposes of analysis, rationalization, and reasoning belongs to the mutable signs. The mutable cross allows us to analyze the various components of a situation, to measure and compare them to a standard or model of experience, to rationalize a sequence of actions, and then to formulate a conclusion. The scientific processes of collecting, analyzing, and classifying data, performing tests, and creating models of reality from tests and observations, as well as the process of acquiring, recording, and storing knowledge, are mutable activities. Based on models and acquired knowledge, we are able to make reasonable assumptions about life, which allows for the furthering of knowledge and the human experience.

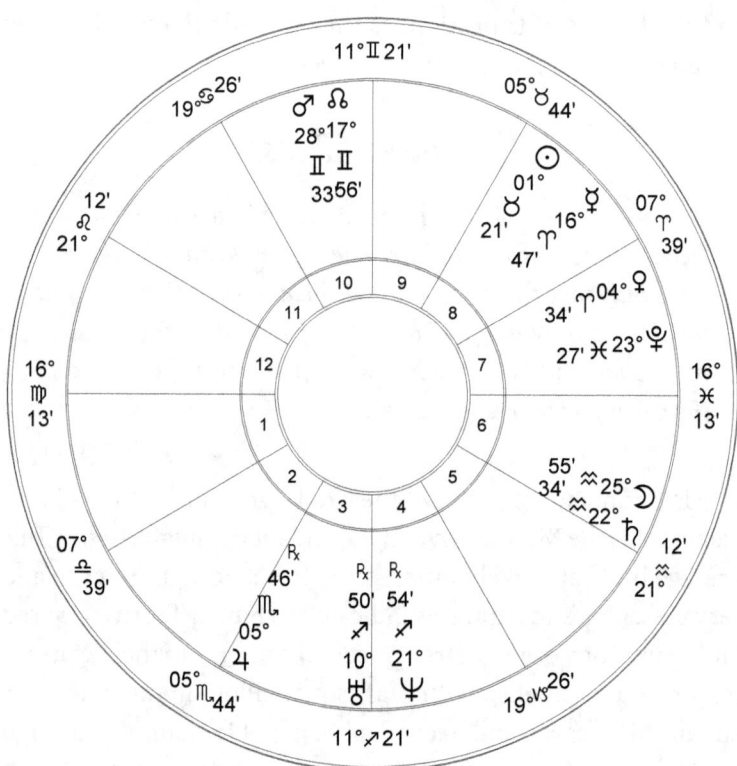

Charlotte Brontë
April 21, 1816

The Mutable Cross

Individuals whose charts contain a strong mutable influence will tend to think things through before acting, unlike their cardinal counterparts who might act before thinking, and their fixed counterparts who might wait until they have to act before doing so. Even if they act quickly or seem to act impulsively, as some mutables can, they usually have had sufficient time to make a qualified evaluation and judgment of the situation. When they become involved in risky activities or activities of questionable value, it is not the result of their having foolishly or mindlessly given in to an impulse. Mutables will usually have a reason for doing what they do, even if it does not seem apparent on the outside. By the same token, they will expect others to be able to justify their own actions with equal reasoning ability.

"The only business of the head in the world is to bow a ceaseless obeisance to the heart."
—W. B. Yeats

"I hate reasonable people," Yeats wrote, explaining his dislike for the novelist George Eliot; *"the activity of their brains sucks up all the blood out of their hearts."*

Interestingly, as in Charlotte Brontë's chart, we find a Mutable-Fixed combination, and again, a desire-reason tension, or the pull between head and heart. The fixed signs here reveal strong feelings, in this case a rather strong expression of dislike for that which is reasonable, an integral part of the poet's own nature, being a native of the mutable sign Gemini.

Mutables can spend a lot of time analyzing a situation or problem to arrive at an acceptable and rational conclusion before taking action; in fact, they sometimes can become so entangled in the process of analysis that they lose touch with the original purpose of the exercise. They can also spend plenty of time talking about doing something or justifying why they have or have not done something, and anyone listening to this mental fencing match (because for the most part, this is what it is) will have a hard time finding fault with the reasoning that has led to the current situation, usually a standstill. Mutables become quite adept at the art of justification, and usually have a ready answer to questions such as, "Why don't you . . . ?" or, "Why did you . . . ?" A typical mutable response begins with, "Yes, but that's because . . ."

Excessive rationalization can keep the mutable signs so busy that they forget or postpone that which the original rationalization process was intended to clarify. Some mutables, especially in the face of a decision that may lead them into the unknown, may, in fact, consciously or unconsciously remain in the rationalization process because it is a familiar and safe place to be. It is an environment that remains within the realm of their control. Sometimes, analysis is better than action and its resulting consequences. This procrastination is sometimes spurred by a fear of being criticized or judged by others or by a refusal to accept responsibility for the outcome of these actions. It may also be born of a fear of "doing the wrong thing."

> "The trouble with Reason is that it becomes meaningless at the exact point where it refuses to act."
>
> —Bernard Devoto

When trapped in the rationalization process, mutables need to be reminded that the brain, when engaged in a mental process of analysis, is but a tool to be used by the self, and contrary to what may be actually occurring, the self is not a slave of the mind. Part of the reason why mutables become trapped in the mental wheel of analysis is that they want very much to do the right thing. If they could, they would ask for guarantees that whatever they undertake will actually be right, correct and successful. On this matter, I have found that women are much more susceptible than men; they will sometimes not move at all until they have some form of guarantee or promise that what they are doing is good, or they will move or affect the necessary changes in their lives only after their safety or the safety of their family has been threatened or compromised.

The Model

During Bériault's discussion of the crosses, mutability was readily associated with the notion of good and evil, given the generally accepted dualistic nature of these signs. But the question remained, good or evil according to what? Or to whom? Implicit in the concept of good and bad is the standard according to which a person or thing is measured, and an important part of the mutable process involves the establishment of these standards.

The development of models is not limited to the world of science; in fact, all facets of the life experience that can be observed, recorded, measured, and communicated can be subjected to this process. We've all been measured against dozens of standards throughout our lives; for example, reading and arithmetic tests in grade school, height and weight charts throughout childhood, driver's education exams, job applications, highway speed traps, IQ tests, cholesterol and blood pressure tests, and mammograms, all of which allow us to determine how we rate according to established standards or rules and whether or not corrections or modifications are required. Pass the drivers ed exam, and you're given a license to drive; drive through a red light, and you'll get a ticket; fail the health exam, and you may require medical treatment.

Standards and rules are established in part to help guide us through life, and to help make the experience smoother and easier to manage. Other standards are based on cultural and religious notions, many of which were developed to normalize the behaviour of individual members of the group. Conform to the tenets of your group and you will be accepted and allowed membership; deviate and you could be reprimanded or even banished. Although rules are sometimes used to control the behaviour of individuals, for the most part they are used to facilitate the social experience.

The elaboration of models is not limited to social, religious, scientific, professional, or otherwise external authorities; individuals determine their own models of reality, based on personal experience and knowledge. For example, a person may have a mental picture of the "perfect mate," and this model will be held up each time someone new is dated. A person who has experienced difficulties in past relationships will grow to expect similar experiences in future relationships. Sometimes people will borrow models of behaviour from someone they idolize or respect, and although imitation may be a great form of flattery, it suggests something about the imitator. The imitation may be a result of a lack of personal talent or ability, or a lack of confidence and sense of self-worth.

Sometimes imitation can be a stepping stone to finding a personal style. Most of us go through such a stage during adolescence by adopting certain dress codes and joining special interest groups. How many parents have cried in shock and disbelief when they were made aware of behaviour that was unbecoming of their cherished offspring? "But that's impossible, not my son," a parent will cry, "he's never that brash." And the distraught parent may be right in that this is not the normal behaviour for John Junior, and John Junior may be as surprised at himself as are his parents at this temporary deviation from his personal norm. Temporary aberrations of behaviour are part of the learning and growing process, and we have all experienced them in one form or another.

People who are strongly marked by the mutable signs and who have only a weakly defined sense of self will tend to act according to an adopted standard in the hope of being rewarded with acceptance and the safety of belonging to a group. The actual nature of the chosen standard of behaviour or belief system will be determined by the person's education, degree of maturity, and strength of character. A strong and confident character with sufficient life experience will develop his own set of standards according to which decisions will be made and experiences will be measured. A weak character, lacking in a sense of self, will adopt, whether consciously or not, a set of standards that originates outside himself, and in so doing, may adopt a set of values that does not favour his own development: "I do things this way because it is the way my mother taught me, it is the way it is supposed to be done, it's the right way to do things," sometimes despite his own natural inclinations.

With the help of marketing tools and techniques, the 1980s and 1990s gave birth to a plethora of classifications and categories (mutable processes) for just about all types of human experience, making it easy for people to bypass their own perceptions (fixed cross) and to judge people, places, and circumstances by sometimes superficial means. "Oh, you're a Gen-Xer; you have no hope in life.... You're a baby-boomer, therefore you are selfish and suffer from avid consumerism, a backlash of your days as a hippy.... I'm a type A...," etc. These are without a doubt interesting sociological and psychological classifications and are helpful in many circumstances, such as when determining pricing strategies for marketing new products, but when it comes to individuals, prefabricated models should not take the place of information derived from one's direct perception. The application of models to make assumptions about people breaks down as a system of information when it completely overrides the use of perception to identify individual differences. In fact, sweeping generalizations can result in misinformation and errors in judgment.

Mutables are more likely than the other crosses to accept or reject a thing, concept, or person based on reputation. "This brand of toothpaste has always had an excellent reputation; This new product by the same company should be really good." For the mutable sign, reputation indicates a proven track record. This is true of many products which have withstood the test of time, we know they are effective or that they will meet the average standard of quality, otherwise no one would purchase them and we would not hear about them. This permits us to bypass the testing phase and go straight to the consuming phase. And this is good, for we certainly do not want to start applying tests to all available variations of a product.

> "When you are courting a nice girl an hour seems like a second. When you sit on a red-hot cinder a second seems like an hour. That's relativity."
>
> —Albert Einstein

It is interesting to note that after Albert Einstein, a native of the mutable sign Pisces, graduated from the Polytechnic Institute in Zurich, he worked in the Swiss patent office in Bern, a job that consisted of verifying technical descriptions in the applications for patents, a very mutable occupation indeed. He found great interest in *looking over inventor's models*. He enjoyed reading and discussing scientific matters with his few friends and was determined to understand how the universe works. Mutable signs often make excellent mechanics, teachers, technicians, and scientists. They have a keen interest in understanding how things work and how people behave. Their inquisitiveness and ability to relate information fosters their ability to teach and to communicate this knowledge to others.

Mutables will test people and things to see if they conform to their idea of what or how they should be. Following a talk I gave some years ago at a local bookstore, I was approached by an woman who began to ask questions that seemed a little strange at the time, given that I had just given a talk on the subject of divination and forecasting. She wanted to know if I was able to tell, from reading a chart, what had happened in a person's life. She was friendly, confident, and articulate in style and appeared to have some basic knowledge of astrology. She indicated that she was not interested in knowing the future, but wanted to know if I could read the past. I explained that I did consider the past in the course of an astrological analysis, but that most clients were more interested in understanding the present and planning for the future. She persisted with her questioning, insisting on knowing how much I could tell about her past. A little surprised by the line of questioning, I asked why she would want to pay for such a service. She replied that she wanted to know if what I would say were true. I asked if she was a mutable sign, perhaps Sagittarius or Virgo. Rather taken by surprise, she replied that she was a Sagittarius and immediately wanted to know how I was able to guess her sign. By her line of questioning, I knew that she was testing me, which is a mutable approach. It was nothing personal, really.

As a general rule, people are likely to respond to given situations in a predictable manner, and mutable signs are very adept at developing an understanding of human behaviour. The error lies in making unqualified assumptions regarding another person without verifying the facts with direct perception, which again is the quick and easy way of doing things: observe and perceive, develop a model, and apply it to situations as they arise. The ideal process requires a verification of the model before it is applied, this takes a little more effort. To the insecure mutable, a behaviour pattern that deviates from the norm may threaten the status quo, which in turn may create inner conflict. Depending on the need for security, the mutable person will have a greater or lesser need for conformity. When very insecure, he will try to convince others that his way is the only right way. This can lead to external conflict as the mutable person attempts to control the responses of his environment. If unsuccessful in his attempts to either convert or control the delinquent behaviour, he may ultimately choose to end the troubling relationship. The secure mutable individual will not feel threatened by differing and even opposing models of reality, but will accept and even welcome them as an integral part of the diversity of the human experience.

Socialization and Communication

> *"Transport of the mails, transport of the human voice, transport of flickering pictures—in this century as in others our highest accomplishments still have the single aim of bringing men together."*[3]
>
> —Antoine de Saint-Exupéry

The mutable signs are essentially the connectors of society, the glue that binds people, situations, ideas, and societies together. They are the people who know people, the friends who can put you in touch with someone who can help you. The mutable points and planetary positions in the chart indicate the development of social and interactive skills. The more mutable points there are, the greater the need for social interaction. Mutable placements show areas where it is important for you to connect via some form of communication with something or someone that is external to you. This communication provides validation to the experience, which otherwise would never become externalized. Who has not run to the telephone when struck by an exciting new idea, eager to share it with a close friend or family member?

Part of the process of relating to something or to someone requires that the thing or person be given a name. Once the situation, thing, or person has a name, it can then be related to others. The New Lexicon Webster's Encyclopedic Dictionary of the English language defines language as "the organized system of speech used by human beings as a means of communication among themselves," (Canadian Edition, Lexicon Publications, Inc. New York 1988) which is clearly a mutable tool. The *naming* of a thing, person, process, or situation, enables us to articulate and share what is occurring or what has been experienced. This ability to relate experiences, to communicate and interact,

---

3. Although a native of the cardinal sign Cancer, Saint-Exupéry had five planets (three of which were in the Midheaven) plus the Ascendant in mutable signs.

contributes to the learning process and to the development of intelligence. Look to the mutable points, house cusps, and planetary placements in your own chart for indications of how and where you relate to the outside world, for areas that might prove to be worthwhile avenues of study or areas that may help you more effectively communicate your inner feelings and desires.

Jones describes the mutable signs as being the Humanistic Temperament, "...as those whose interests are centered in direct and highly personal relations with others. The humanistic type is highly sensitive to group evaluation of any sort and in consequence he carries the whole weight of his own being around with him wherever he goes.... He is a great joiner and follower in life, always desiring to be a definite part of things."

> *"The biggest disease today is not leprosy or tuberculosis, but rather the feeling of being unwanted."*
> —Mother Theresa

The dualistic nature of the mutable signs leads to the inclusion of the other in the life experience while creating a need to be included and to belong to something that is external to the self. One of the purposes of communication, other than to exchange and share experiences with others, is to satisfy the need for acceptance and belonging. On a fundamental level, feedback from another person acknowledges one's existence and accords a degree of validation to the experience. Mutables tend to seek validation through acceptance and similitude of experience. They will listen to another person's story and seek a comparable one of their own, following up with, "Yes, and that's just like when I did..." At times, these comparisons may not make sense to the casual observer, who must be very attentive to catch which part or aspect of the experience has been compared. Mutables will relate another person's experience to the models they have created based on their own experience or on accepted convention. Conformity of experience leads to acceptance, brotherhood, sisterhood, fraternization, and hence to a feeling of security. At times, their need to relate and measure up to others may seem like competitive behaviour, but it is really an attempt to validate personal experience, where conformity provides a feeling of acceptance and security.

For the mutable signs, personal value and self-worth are often measured by other people's responses or by their degree of acceptance or rejection. Acceptance is validating and gives meaning to the experience, while rejection is devastating and destroys the value of the experience. In order to gain acceptance, mutables will also try to act in a way that pleases others, or in a way that will elicit a desired response from another person. They can forget their own needs in the process and even lose their identity or allow their identity to become tied into that of another by projection. Insecure mutables will seek to have and maintain relationships because only in this way can they have a sense of who they are; that is, they know themselves by the reactions, input, and feedback of the other people in their lives: "If the other is content, I should be content. If the other is satisfied, he will treat me well. If I please the other, I can make him do as I want." An element of control comes into play in this type of interaction; there are "strings attached" where the other is expected to perform in a predetermined manner. If the desired response is obtained, then the relationship is good; if not, then it is bad.

> *"There is but one love of Jesus, as there is but one person in the poor - Jesus. We take vows of chastity to love Christ with undivided love; to be able to love him with undivided love we take a vow of poverty which frees us from all material possessions, and with that freedom we can love him with undivided love, and from this vow of undivided love we surrender ourselves totally to him in the person who takes his place."*
> —Mother Theresa, *A Gift for God*.

When mutable signs focus on something outside themselves, be it a person, project, or service, this external focus can become the object of their affection, devotion, and/or attention to the exclusion of their own needs. The practice of self-sacrifice is essentially mutable. A prime example of this devotion to service is Mother Theresa, the Catholic missionary who dedicated her life to helping the poor and suffering in India. She was a native of the mutable sign Virgo, with the Moon, Mars, Pluto, and the Ascendant in mutable signs. The strong cardinal showing, four planets plus the Midheaven, gave strength to her convictions and the courage and drive to carry out her humanitarian mission.

Depending on the individual's degree of selflessness, there will be a greater or lesser degree of attachment or expectation associated with the act of giving. In a truly selfless act, the giving will have no strings attached; that is, it becomes an act of unconditional love. If the giving is not selfless, there will be expectations of return on the investment of time, emotions, and money or energy, which will be easily recognizable by the significant number of "strings attached."

Everyone is subject to the occasional bout of projection, but those whose charts are marked by significant mutable placements are more susceptible to indulging in this practice. By contrast, the fixed signs are more likely to absorb responsibility for situations rather than to project it externally. In fact, strongly fixed persons are sometimes overburdened by responsibility that does not belong to them simply because of the fact that they have difficulty accepting that there is a reality outside themselves and that responsibilities can be shared. When mutables take on the responsibilities of others, it is the result of a more conscious choice, usually out of a need to relate, a need to feel needed by others, which in turn gives purpose to their lives. In situations of denial, mutables can become very creative in the justification of their behaviour and choices, but they can also tend to look for an external cause for their problems and find a way of pointing a finger away from themselves. "The devil made me do it" is easier to accept than "I made a mistake," which really means "I could not live up to my own standards and so I have to find someone else to blame."

ASTROLOGICAL CROSSES

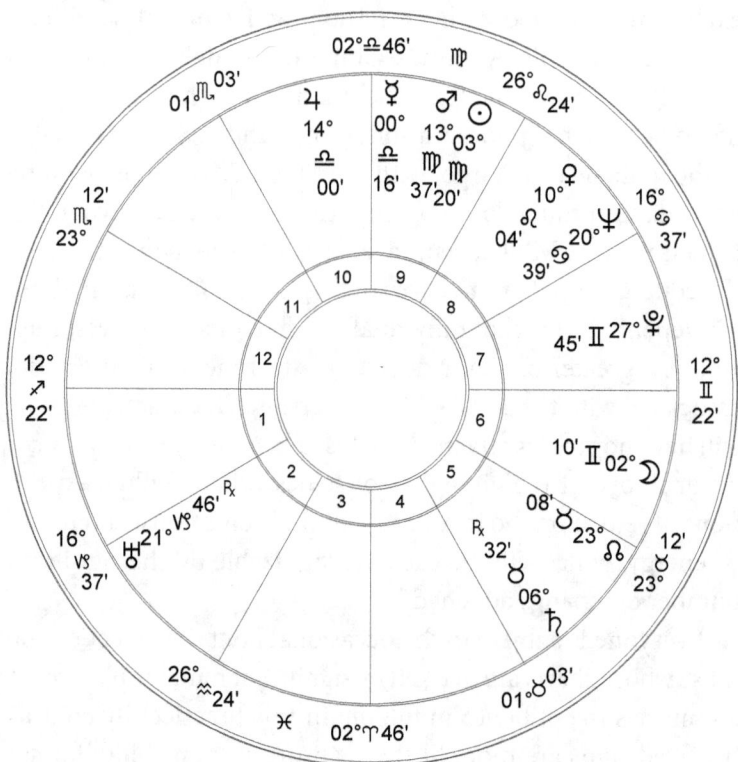

Mother Teresa
August 27, 1910 (birthdate unconfirmed)

The Mutable Cross

Mutable individuals tend to think and act for those in their care, or for whom they are responsible. They will assume that what is good for them should also be good for the other. In this way, the mutable natives act not only to satisfy their own desires and inclinations, but also to satisfy those of another person. This is the basis of the mutable sign's ability to know and understand the needs of others. The mutable response in a situation that involves another might be thus: "I feel this way about this turn of events. Based on what I know, this seems to be the normal type of response for this situation, therefore the other person should and must also be feeling the same way." This poses no problem as long as the other person is, in fact, responding according to the norm on which the assumption is based. The mutable individual would then proceed with the assumption and act accordingly. If your best friend has a cold, and your standard family remedy is chicken soup, you won't think twice about bringing over a pot of hot soup to help your friend get better more quickly.

However, by its very nature, looking out for another necessitates the making of an assumption about the other person or about the other person's needs. Sometimes the assumption can be tainted by a projection of one's own fears, needs, and feelings, rendering the basic assumption false, resulting in inappropriate action being taken insofar as the other person is concerned. This can lead to the other person feeling misunderstood or even alienated, depending on the degree of inaccuracy of the assumption made in his regard. For example, a mutable person calls a fixed-sign friend who is alone on a Saturday night, while everyone is getting ready to go out and have a good time. "Why don't you join us?" says the mutable to the fixed friend, meaning, "You must be sad or lonely. I would be if I were in your position. Please come out with us so you won't be alone." The fixed friend, who has had a hellish week dealing with customer requests and problems at work, has been looking forward to that special time alone when he does not have to deal with others on any level. To have someone recognize this fact would make the fixed person feel understood and accepted, while to have someone suggest he behave according to the norm will only add stress.

Sometimes, mutables will justify the behaviour of others, even behaviour that they find to be troubling or disturbing, usually as a way of avoiding direct confrontation. A Pisces client once brought up issues concerning her relationship with her Gemini boss. She felt that he tended to control her work too closely, hampering her ability to be creative and productive; in fact, she felt as though he wanted her to be an extension of him, to do his work in his place. I suggested that she might want to find a nice way to express her concerns before too much stress had accumulated. Her response was to excuse his behaviour, saying that he was such a nice guy. The significant source of problems in this relationship was the mutable tendency to seek control, as was manifested by her mutable boss.

Control of issues, circumstances, and people is an important way in which mutable signs garner power, and their relational abilities make it easy for them to obtain power this way. Being in control also increases the chances that things will go a certain way, the right way, *the way I want them to go*, thereby providing some level of guarantee. Queen Elizabeth was certainly empowered by the fact that she had a say in who she would or would not marry. Her ability to control this aspect of her life kept the persons in positions of power in her country and abroad guessing, a level of control that she probably exercised with a certain relish.

Mutables can put up with abusive behaviour in personal relationships because of a deep-seated need to be in a relationship at all costs. They will find ways of excusing negative and even harmful behaviour, giving themselves a reason to stick it out just a little while longer, avoiding the inevitable confrontation and ultimately delaying the breakup of the relationship. There is no reasoning with mutable individuals trapped in such a situation, for they will have a reason or answer for every point you bring up; in fact, this is part of their problem—they talk themselves into staying in the negative situation.

The Mutable Cross

Mutable individuals have the charming and friendly way of using names to define the subjects of their conversations, and very often there are several subjects included in these conversations. Everyone has picked up the phone and heard, "Hi, it's Steve." Normally, this would not pose a problem unless you happen to be acquainted with five Steves. Also, they will extend this social courtesy by using the names of third parties of whom they are speaking, regardless of whether or not their interlocutor is familiar with these persons. For someone with little mutable representation in their natal chart, it becomes an intellectual juggling act trying to attach relevant information to the names so as to have points of reference when these are referred to in the course of a conversation. Some years ago, I helped my Sagittarian friend James update and print his curriculum vitae for a new job application. I couldn't help but notice that he had two full pages of references, including names, titles, and phone numbers, to one page of work experience. Clearly he valued his contacts over his work experience. Eventually he did land a job, an excellent one at that, and this, not surprisingly, through the contacts he had made in the work field.

Going back to our astrology conference interviews, it now becomes quite clear to which cross the first person interviewed belongs. The human connection, the diversity of the experience and the element of communication, all mutable factors, are clearly indicated in this person's response.

> "I asked her why she thought the conference experience was important. 'It's important because there are so many different ways of looking at astrology, so many different views and methods and ideas. Conferences provide an excellent way to exchange our ideas and to get to know each other personally, to get to know the person behind the book, say. And when it's an international conference, you see people from abroad with whom you don't usually get a chance to talk.'"

Growing up Mutable

Parents of mutable children would do well to monitor their responses to their children's behaviour, for these children will act very much according to how he interprets the reactions of teachers, parents, and mentors. These children are very Pavlovian. They are easier to control than cardinal or fixed children in that a positive word of encouragement or a promise of a reward will go a long way in reinforcing behaviour. Their parents need to be aware of what they find "cute" in their young children, for this behaviour will be repeated for a long time.

On the other hand, a lack of response from the parent or guardian, as in the case of a parent who is absent, or even just too busy or preoccupied, will cause deep wounds in the child, where the absence will be interpreted as exclusion and rejection. They will seek to fit in somewhere else, even if this other environment might ultimately have harmful effects. For these youngsters, to feel included in a group or gang, even if the group participates in illicit activities, is better that to be left feeling alone and unwanted at home.

Children who are marked by the mutable cross are generally very communicative. When they talk, they need feedback, because they are testing their ideas against those of the world outside themselves. They will exchange ideas and experiences among each other, comparing notes and choosing from these experiences those which best suit their needs. They are very sensitive and aware of everything that is going on around them. They are "information sponges," intellectually quick, adaptable, and flexible. In a way, these children can be somewhat mercenary in their approach to situations. They will dispassionately (for passion belongs to the cardinal cross) analyze, evaluate, and process information and come up with "the best deal" for themselves. If a certain type of behaviour will get them what they want, then they will act it out that way. They will do what is expected of them, for they have carefully studied the responses of those around them.

The Mutable Cross

Mutable children are great imitators. They can reproduce all forms of reality as it is presented to them. I was a little embarrassed one day when, having decided to take a walk and greet my daughter on her way home from kindergarten, I turned the corner and caught sight of her just a block away. (Caroline has Mercury and Venus in Gemini opposed Moon in Sagittarius.) When she saw me, she suddenly stopped, dropped her school bag, flung her arms up, longingly cried my name, ran toward me and threw her arms about me as though having finally found her long-lost love. The whole episode was most interesting to observe, considering the level of drama of the scene, but without the required emotional element. She was clearly play-acting. As the school was just three blocks from the house, and we had had lunch together at the house just a couple of hours earlier, I gathered that she was trying out a response she had seen on television the night before.

Some mutable children will behave according to the rules, or as they are "supposed to," like mother or father does or as they were told they should. For example, a young girl might take her mother's recipe and bake a batch of cookies as instructed. The cookies should taste good, because they did when mother made them, and they were made as mother made them. She won't taste them and judge for herself. Mutable children will dress the doll to look like she does in the picture on the box, or they will arrange the farm animals as they are supposed to be in "real life."

Mutable children is most likely to conform in order to be included in the group. Peer pressure is strongly felt here. They are the adolescents who are most likely to "need" those designer jeans at twice the price of regular jeans. Parents who object to these children's apparently "outrageous" demands do not understand the importance of this very real need to feel included. For mutable adolescents, it is useless to try to reason that a designer label does not warrant the cost of the jeans. To these adolescents, it is a matter of survival, since if they cannot conform, they will lose their status in the group and thus be excluded from that which gives them a sense of identity — the group. It is better to suggest that it might be time to find a part-time job so they can purchase their own designer clothes. Ask them what their friends do for pocket money. Maybe they can do the same.

This need for conformity will only be overridden if a strong security base is established early in life. If mutable children feel safe and secure and are well integrated in the family group, they will be able later on to experiment with other forms of reality. They will be able to weigh the pressure of the group versus their own need to innovate, and perhaps may allow themselves to try something new. But this will happen only if they do not fear exclusion by judgement. If they have been brought up to accept the occasional failure as a normal part of life, they will expand their field of activity to include that which is outside the normal sphere of experience. But if they think they might be rejected if they behave differently, or that they might be judged harshly if they fail, they will not venture far from the norm. For them, it is better to be "like everyone else" than to risk being different and marginal. The thought of being alone and isolated can be a horrifying experience for the mutable sign. The strong and confident mutable child will take pleasure in exploring many different facets of life.

5

The Crosses in the Life Experience

Several years ago, I was home sick with a very bad case of the flu. It was probably bronchitis, but as a fixed sign, I wanted to deal with it in my own way; besides, I rarely go to the doctor. So I took to mixing my own herbs, made teas, ate lots of garlic, and generally tired myself out trying to heal myself; such is the nature of the fixed signs. They rarely take advice from others, and you are likely to hear them say, "I'll do it myself. I don't need anybody." When ill, they prefer to burrow under the covers and wait for the symptoms to pass, like an injured animal might do.

    I was just falling asleep when the telephone rang. A concerned cardinal friend was calling to see how I was faring. I described my symptoms, and the treatments I had prescribed for myself. Horrified, she quickly responded with, "You should go to the doctor. You can't diagnose yourself like that. You aren't a doctor." I smiled to myself, and to quiet her concerns, agreed to go to a clinic in a few days if I was not successful with my own ministrations. Cardinal signs will consult an *authority* rather than trust their own *perceptions* (fixed). "The doctor knows." They will believe in the doctor because of the established, recognized, and accepted power of that profession. I managed to fall asleep that morning, only to be awakened by the ring of the phone once again. This time, it was my mutable friend.

"Have you tried thyme?" she said quickly.

"No, I'm all out. But I'm using elder and mint."

"I'll bring you some. How about..."

It soon became clear to me that it would be of no use to try to stop her. I just wanted to return to bed, and contemplated disconnecting the intrusive telephone. Soon, my friend was at the door with a grocery bag full of remedies and the proper food I was apparently not getting into me. The ever-helpful *relating* nature of the mutable sign led her to *experiment* with her techniques. Anyway, I got a millet loaf, some more herbs, and a massage from that encounter.

It should be added here that both these individuals have more than just the Sun in their respective crosses; in fact, the crosses in question are quite strong in each chart. By the way, I did manage to finally curl up in my bed, get some sleep, and overcome my illness. And I did it in my own, fixed way: slowly and alone. Clearly in this situation, each cross responded in a unique way, each wanting to find a solution and to be of help. In recognizing the essential differences between the crosses, it becomes easier to understand and to accept the behaviour of others, perhaps even enabling us to appreciate the diversity in our experiences.

In the process of analyzing a birth chart, a careful study of the cross distribution as well as key placements of planetary configurations will provide essential information about basic character, strengths, talents, inner motivation, personal style, and probable and potential problematic areas. Significant cross placements can reveal why certain life decisions have been made or why certain areas of activity have been favoured over others. For example, a strong cardinal showing in a chart will often indicate a need for personal power and a talent for building, hence an inclination for business or engineering, while a strongly mutable chart will indicate analytical or communication skills, inclining the native

The Crosses in the Life Experience

to the social sciences or education. By itself, the cross distribution in a chart can indeed be very revealing.

Cross interpretation need not be limited to planetary distribution and preponderance, but can also be considered in terms of a complete process, regardless of whether or not one cross dominates or another is absent in the chart. In most life projects or enterprises, the energy of each of the three crosses is required at one stage or another if the undertaking is to reach completion. Cardinal energy provides the initial idea, the germ from which is born that which is to be realized in some near or distant future. It nurtures ambition and provides the impetus for moving forward. Cardinal energy stimulates imagination and generates the drive to overcome inertia; and also provides the courage to face the unknown. Improperly channelled cardinal energy can become dispersed in non-productive or even destructive activities, or can sustain self-delusion and impractical fantasy.

Fixed-sign energy allows for the experience to be put into a context, to be established in a reality and to be given a valid and viable form, assuring that the original ideal ultimately reaches fruition. Fixed energy gives value to the experience and seeks to ensure and maximize the rewards of the experience while minimizing its costs and losses. It also provides the creativity and the drive to produce and to accomplish tangible results, as well as the stamina and staying power to do what needs to be done to achieve these results. The plan reaches the stage of production. With insufficient or unavailable fixed energy, that is, fixed energy that has been blocked by feelings of inadequacy, low self-esteem or lack of self confidence, a project can long remain in the realm of the idea or the dream. Also, with insufficient fixed energy there can be a lack of a sense of worth for the project, diminishing the motivation to bring it to completion and the desire to see it made real. Blocked fixed energy can sometimes become obsessed with achieving a product of an unreasonable and even unattainable degree of perfection.

The mutable signs provide the connections that are required during the development of the project, allowing otherwise unrelated elements to come together in a cohesive process. Mutable energy favours communication and enables the swift transmission of essential information between parties. This cross also facilitates the development and propagation of knowledge by establishing patterns and models from the experience, enabling others to repeat the experience with fewer challenges and greater ease. In this way, the entire process gains significance in that it can be understood and repeated by others. Mutable energy may be reflected in the initial phase as the justification or rationalizing for the project. Mutability will also ensure that the result conforms to the original idea or plan, or conforms to norms and specification, and will recommend modifications to the process if required. Insufficient mutable energy can result in an inability to learn from the experience, an inability to apply knowledge, or a failure to effectively communicate essential information. Blocked mutable energy can slow down or even prevent a project from getting underway by falling into the trap of incessant analysis, "analyze and paralyze," often caused by a deep fear of not measuring up to standards or fear of losing control of circumstances judged to be essential.

As a simple example, we can see the role played by each cross in a project which involves the decoration of a room. The initial idea, the enthusiasm for change, the blueprint, and the plan will be animated by cardinal energy. The mutable cross allows us to rationalize the project and then to use existing resources and knowledge, perhaps by prompting a call to a friend from whom we can get advice about decoration. Fixed energy will fuel the desire to see the project completed, as well as veer the project toward a product or result that will also deliver pleasure and satisfaction. The purchasing and gathering of resources, tools, and equipment and the actual work will be determined by fixed energy. Verification of the result to determine whether or not it conforms to the original idea, as well as approval, "This is good," or disapproval, "This is not good enough," will belong to the mutable cross. The mutable aspect of the project will let us also derive knowledge from the experience.

Depending on cross distribution in the natal chart, a person may be more at ease with one aspect of the project than with others. Being motivated and getting started will be more difficult if there is a lack of cardinal representation. Seeing the project through to completion might be a challenge without sufficient fixed energy. A lack of mutable energy may present a problem on a communication or knowledge level, or may prevent the person from accepting the possibility of alternate options or approaches in addressing obstacles, resulting in a lack of flexibility and perhaps missed opportunities. Being aware of our cross distribution and any associated weakness or lack, we can then apply extra attention or request help in the areas which might otherwise prove to be problematic.

A client once brought to my attention an observation she had made while completing studies at university. It would appear that students were divided in their facility for learning the various sciences so that those who had a talent for chemistry usually had a harder time with math and physics, and those who had an easy time with math usually had a talent for physics but had a harder time with chemistry. This led me to do a little digging among my client files, where I found this observation to be consistent with what I associated with the crosses: mutable signs tend toward chemistry, the cardinals toward mathematics, physics and engineering, while the fixed signs seem to be drawn toward human and animal biology. This indicates that there may be a difference in the way the human brain functions from one cross to the next.

Another observation I have made over the years is that the mutable signs, especially Virgo and Sagittarius,, tend to be partial to dogs as pets, while the fixed signs tend to favour cats. No preference was noted among the cardinal signs. In a way, this is in keeping with the strong social aspect of the mutable signs;

dog people are known for their sociable and gregarious natures and will often be seen chatting with other dog owners as they go about their daily walks. Cat people, well, they either act as jailer, limiting their treasured pets to the confines of their indoor palace, or they act as doormen, catering to the their aloof pet's mood for fresh air, garden mischief, and affection. A friend described how her daughter had harnessed her aging cat with a collar and leash while on vacation so that he could be taken out for walks. Only a mutable sign could buckle a cat into a leash, I thought, and as it turned out, the daughter was a mutable native, with six mutable planets.

Cross Pairings

Cross pairings can provide interesting information about individual potential and character type. The cardinal-fixed combination for example is a busy and productive combination. The chart of Odile is an excellent example of this type of combination, one who would rather work than talk. These people are driven by a need for concrete accomplishment (fixed) combined with a desire to achieve some level of worldly success (cardinal). Henry Ford is another example, with four fixed and four cardinal planets, this man was a real workhorse. He even came out of retirement at the age of 80 to run the company after his son died, and ran it for two years until his grandson became president of the manufacturing company.

> "I have a dream. It is a dream deeply rooted in the American dream…a dream that my four little children will one day live in a nation where they will not be judged by the color of their skin but by the content of their character."
>
> —Dr. Martin Luther King Jr.

The cardinal-mutable combination is dynamic and often involved in social and political activities. Many writers have the cardinal-mutable combination, including Antoine de Saint

The Crosses in the Life Experience

Exupéry, Paolo Coehlo, Charles Beaudelaire, Barbara Cartland, Stephen King, George Orwell, Sir Richard Burton, and Ernest Hemingway. These individuals will tend to do things for others or with others in mind. They can set aside the self and may even lose their true sense of personal value in their service to, and involvement with, others. The chart of Martin Luther King is an excellent example of how personal power can be expressed when cardinal and mutable energies are combined and applied toward the accomplishment of a specific goal. Here was a middle-class black man who, although he had not suffered the plight of many of his race, was willing to embrace a cause (cardinal) that served (mutable) to benefit others (mutable). Not only was he a man of deep and passionate convictions (cardinal Sun), he was also willing to sacrifice himself (mutable) for the cause in which he believed (cardinal). His philosophy, based on the teachings of Gandhi and Jesus, was founded on principles of nonviolence and love, strong ideals indeed, given the socio-political challenges faced by the SCLC (Southern Christian Leadership Conference), the organization of which he was made leader (cardinal). "We will match your capacity to inflict suffering with our capacity to endure suffering...," he said to those who opposed the efforts of the SCLC. The Moon (unconscious desires) and Venus (personal values) being in mutable signs, combined with Mercury (mind and communication ability) in the air sign Aquarius and on the Midheaven provided a very strong talent for communication. He no doubt was a man of great knowledge who was able to organize (Mercury in the fixed sign of Aquarius at the Midheaven) this knowledge in a way that gave him broad human appeal (Aquarius). This cardinal-mutable combination was expressed by a man of power, vision, and remarkable ability as an orator.

The mutable-fixed combination reflects the tendency to be very attentive to detail, sometimes painfully critical, but mostly this is the combination of the born perfectionist. Martha Stewart, a native of the fixed sign Leo, is one such individual, very productive, creative, and attentive to detail. Her chart includes four fixed

ASTROLOGICAL CROSSES

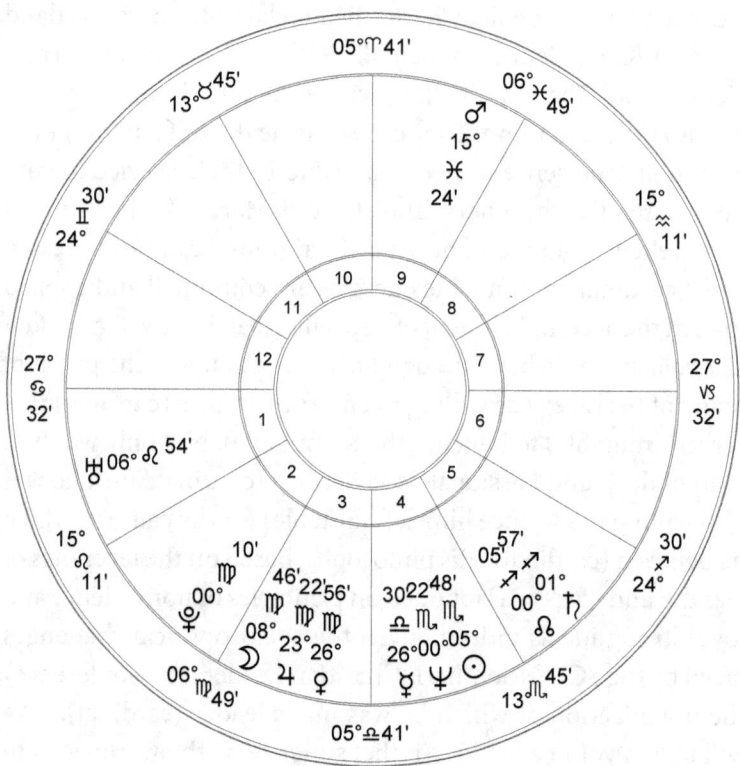

Bill Gates
October 28, 1956

and four mutable planets. Another prime example of this tendency to perfectionism is the chart of performer-creator Barbra Streisand, well known for her demanding creative nature. Another example of the fixed-mutable combination is Bill Gates, with four fixed and six mutable planets. His fixed energy drove him to seek, at any price, what he desired (fixed), which was to become a major player in a burgeoning new industry, while his mutable energy provided him with the ability to finesse his way through the significant negotiations that would ultimately completely alter the course of the information technology industry.

In the movie *Pirates of Silicon Valley*, which recounts the story of Bill Gates, Steve Wozniac, and Steve Jobs, Gates is quoted as saying, "You know how you survive? You make people need you. You survive because you make them need what you have, and then they have nowhere else to go." These words immediately capture the mutable strength of this chart, and indeed, this is how he obtained his big break. IBM needed an operating system for its PC in order to compete with Apple. Gates found an operating system that no one wanted to buy, owned by a small, unknown computer company in Seattle. He saw an opportunity, connected the two, purchased the software, negotiated a deal with IBM, developed the product that met the need, and the rest is history.

Steve Jobs was making history too, but his style was completely different. A native of the mutable sign Pisces, with no other mutable planets and with six cardinal planets (as compared to only one in Gate's chart), Jobs was a much more colourful character, portrayed in the same movie as a man in search of greatness for whom the development of his business was more akin to a religious experience, at one point proclaiming that "everyone needs a cause," a very cardinal point of view. Given his strong cardinal energy, he became carried away by the glory of his newfound fame and fortune and even saw "karma and the meaning of the universe" in his flourishing enterprise.

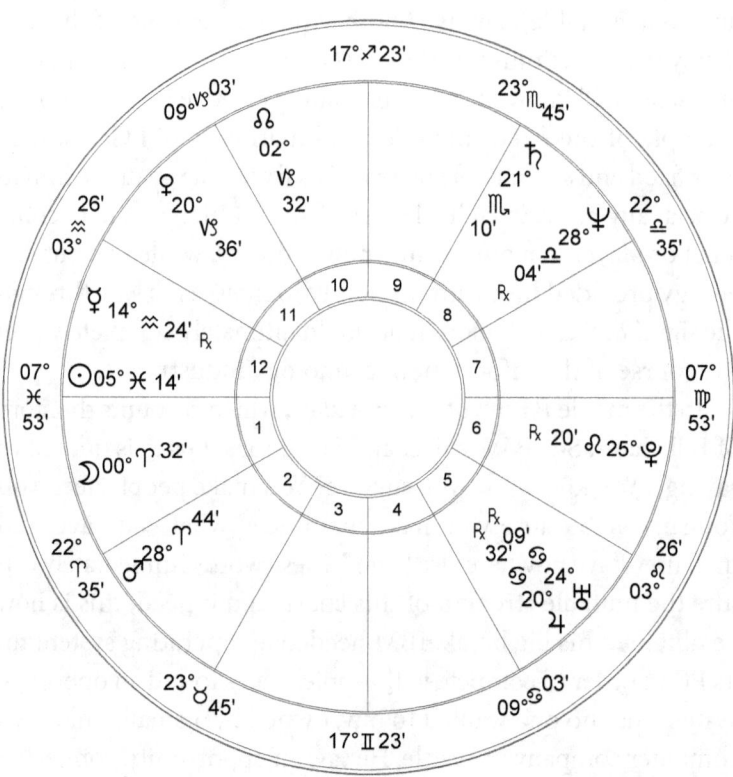

Steve Jobs
February 24, 1956

The Crosses and Transit Periods

In addition to natal chart disposition, transits and progressions should be considered in the analysis of an individual's situation. A series of cardinal transits, for example, could put the emphasis on the need for action, the need to find a new direction in life, a new goal, or to take initiative in an area that has consistently been relegated to the "I'll-do-it-later" pile. Cardinal energy brings up questions such as *Where do I want to go next? What are my plans for the future? Do my previous ideals still apply? What are my goals? What motivates me? What drives me to pursue my current activities? How much power do I have in the determination of my life experiences? How can I make a difference in the world? What significance does my function have in the overall scheme of things?*

Transits in fixed signs might underline the importance of production or creativity, of results, self-worth, and the value of one's life experience. *Who am I?* is a very fixed question, and for many people, especially those who define themselves by the response elicited by others, such as the mutables, this can prove to be a painful and confusing transit. A Pisces client (four planets mutable, including the Sun and Moon) complained about how difficult a time he was having while Jupiter and Saturn transited his eighth house and Neptune and Uranus transited his fourth house setting off a series of conjunctions, squares and oppositions to his four fixed natal planets. What troubled him most was having to reevaluate his set of personal values. He found it very difficult to identify and express what really mattered to him in life. His decisions for the future depended on his ability to face himself, a reality check which he found to be a laborious and distressing exercise. He was becoming more intolerant of work that had no value-added benefits (fixed), yet at the same time he continued to put a tremendous amount of stress on himself to perform according to expectations (mutable). During these transits, he focused on what he lacked, a negative fixed manifestation, rather than on his acquired knowledge and past experience. The fact that he was well respected by his superiors did nothing to subdue his lack of self-confidence, and his negative perception of himself caused him to be hesitant in taking steps forward.

Fixed transits put the emphasis on values and on results. *What is the value of my current job situation? Do I really like it? Is it truly satisfactory? Is it meeting my real, current needs? Does it reflect my present reality?* A difficult and improperly managed fixed transit can lead to depression, hopelessness, confrontation with self, and diminished self-esteem. These transits can also halt or slow creativity and productivity as well as generate doubt in the value of one's work. Fixed-transit periods can be solitary times, where there is a deep need for solitude. A distressed fixed person is akin to an ailing animal in the wild, preferring to burrow until the healing occurs. The self-reevaluation which usually accompanies the fixed transit is generally not easy to externalize or to put into words. It is an internal process and is easier to express through creative works.

A focus on the mutable signs would naturally bring up relationship issues as well as a need for flexibility and diversity of experience, loosening of controls, improved communication, and learning. *What have I learned from my experiences, and how can I use this to improve my situation? How can I more effectively communicate what I feel or what I want?* These are valid mutable-transit questions. Another area that is likely to be stirred up during a mutable transit is the sense of belonging. *Are my needs for social integration and acceptance being met? Do I feel that I have a safe place in the society or community to which I belong? Do I have people with whom I can share life experiences? Do the people in my life bring me the social and emotional support and stimulation I need?* A series of mutable transits might cause a person to question past decisions. *Why do I do what I do? Am I doing things for the right reasons?*

Communication: Mutable and Air

It may be necessary at this point to establish the difference between the air element and the mutable cross, as they each in some way relate to communication. The air signs generally enjoy the act of communicating and sharing their ideas for its own sake; consequently, they seek the company of others to enable the process to occur. The air element is intellectual and sociable and has a need for intellectual contact, but not necessarily for relational and emotional commitment. Mutable signs need to be in a relationship *with* someone, whether or not they seek to share the expression of thoughts or experiences is not so much an issue as is the fact of *relating*. Mutable-air Gemini is both relational *and* sociable, where the purpose of communicating is to establish relationships and to determine ties, and there is a profound need to be in contact with others. By communicating with another individual, by expressing a thought and sharing experiences, mutable-sign individuals establish a link, or a tie, with that person. By communicating with another individual, air-sign individuals find an avenue of self-expression. The vehicle, communication, is similar, but the perceived result is intrinsically different.

Aquarians are sociable insofar as this provides them with a platform for self-expression. As a fixed sign, Aquarius seeks opportunities to be; as an air sign, Aquarius needs to express that which they know, "I know" being a common key phrase for the sign, knowledge being something of value (fixed) to Aquarius. They do not have as strong a need to be in a constant relationship situation as does Gemini.

As an air sign, Libra enjoys the social spheres of the human experience; however, unlike their mutable and fixed counterparts, Libra natives will seek out companionship in the hope of sharing an experience of love, excitement, enjoyment, etc. The essential goal is different. As a cardinal sign, Libra seeks stimulation and by its relational nature, it seeks to share this with someone else. Libra's thrill is in the sharing, not in the relating: "We can do this together, we enjoy the same foods, we share the same friends." Libras will seek to have and maintain the ideal union, meaning they want to share the experience with someone who shares their passions and ideas.

Suzie's Sun in Libra indicates that she enjoys the company of others, that she has a sociable, outgoing and friendly disposition, and that she is expressive and has lots of charm. By the Sun's placement in the fifth house, she looks for ways to express herself creatively on the one hand and through love relationships on the other. Although it receives a trine from Jupiter and is in mutual reception with Venus, her Sun is stressfully aspected by a quincunx from Saturn and semisquares from both Neptune and Venus. As the fourth-house ruler of foundations and security base, as well as being situated on the Venus-Neptune midpoint and square the Moon-Mercury, Mars-Jupiter and Moon-Pluto midpoints, the Sun is an important focal point of the chart.

With a strong fifth house, including Mercury, the ruler of both the Ascendant and the second house of self-worth, Suzie has spent much of her life in search of love, validation, and acceptance. The strong mutable energy—three of the fifth-house planets are in Virgo, and the Ascendant, North Node, and second-house cusp are in Gemini—indicates a tendency to include "others" in her process of finding a sense of self-worth and self-love. The Venus-Neptune square in fixed signs further emphasizes the confused perception of herself and her need for love. Needless to say, Suzie has experienced some difficult relationship situations in her life. Part of the problem stemmed from the fact that she did not know how to separate herself from the significant other person in her life. She assumed responsibility for the other's decisions and state of mind (mutable) and in so doing, lost her centre of focus. This caused anxiety, tension, and depression, and even a loss of will to deal with the situation. This is a typical mutable problem, one which requires conscious efforts at reestablishing the self's center of focus through healthy self awareness and acceptance.

The Crosses in the Life Experience

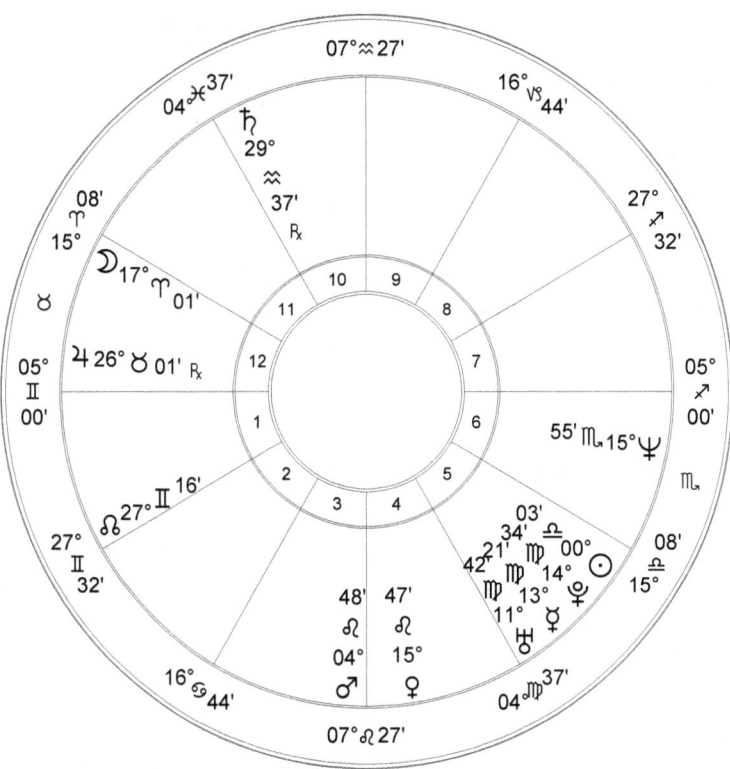

Suzie

Star-Crossed Relationships

Astrological traits often filter down through the generations of a family, and it is interesting to observe the dynamics that occur within this type of nucleus. The predominantly cardinal household is bustling with activity, and sounds can be heard just about everywhere with all manner of radios, stereos, computers, and televisions playing out some form of sensorial stimulus. The fixed household does not seem like a family, for each party is often off doing something on their own. The mutable household is deeply involved in negotiations and discussions, where each is involved in the affairs of another on some level. Look for the black sheep of the family, the one who is very often a member of another cross. This person is likely to connect with the one person who shares planets in his or her cross. A lack of cross connection with a parent makes it difficult for children to express their needs; a lack of self-confidence often results from this inability to communicate. A family member who cannot connect with the family will look outside for this contact, but an external relationship can never completely replace a family connection. A study of the crosses can help improve these relationships by providing insights into the inner workings of each of the individuals concerned.

Nowhere other than in chart comparison (synastry) do the crosses offer more understanding of the mechanisms at work. Years of study and observation have reinforced my conviction that the *crosses*, and not the elements, are the most important factor in determining compatibility in relationships. What popular astrology book does not encourage fire signs to look for another fire sign as a potential ideal life partner? Or earth to find another earth, and air to mate with air? How many rational Sagittarians have been exasperated by irrational Aries impulsiveness, while the same Aries have been annoyed by the Sagittarian's hesitation and lack of action? How many independent Aquarians have felt suffocated and controlled by a well-meaning mother-hen

Gemini, while the Gemini has felt left out in the cold by the non-interference and seeming aloofness of an Aquarian mate?

How much easier for Taurus and Leo to get together and build a garden shed than Leo and Sagittarius, who would end up arguing beauty versus rationalization. Sleeves rolled up, work shoes tightly laced, Taurus and Leo will enjoy getting their hands dirty, cutting the wood, smelling the earth. The whole building process would be a pleasure. They would work in silence, for long periods, simply enjoying the work. Leo and Sagittarius might find themselves discussing the merits of the project, and spend much time rationalizing it from various aspects—value, beauty, positioning, usefulness, so that the project may never get under way.

Most astrologers will agree that it is important to continually adapt astrological interpretations to sociological and cultural changes, and this is very true in the matter of personal relations. The fast-changing world in which we currently live requires that we make adjustments in our way of approaching and analyzing relationships. It would not be fair to the client, nor would an accurate reading be provided, if we were to view relationships with the values of our parents or grandparents. To our elders, who were much more bound by social and religious norms than we are today, a couple married for life, and that was that. If they had irreconcilable differences of character, they never allowed it to become an issue. If one failed to find a comfortable haven for growth and self-expression, this did not become an issue.

Today's youth have been brought up by a generation of individualists, and they have been taught, in turn, to seek to express themselves and to go after what they want. Sex, intimacy, and marriage do not hold the same values they once did. Relationships used to be tied into a life concept that centred around family, survival, loyalty, and security. Relationships today have become another cog in the wheel of life, like the job, the kids that might come one day, going out with friends and having a good time, self-development and uncovering the meaning of life. Today's youth have few, or at least fewer, illusions about married life than the preceding generation, a group lost in the transition between unfailing, deeply entrenched family, religious and marital values and the absence of such in a world where individuality and freedom have become driving forces. Given the importance of the "self" in the new way of perceiving reality and ultimately in the process of designing one's lifestyle, the crosses take on a whole new level of importance, given that they profoundly affect the how and the why of one's actions.

In the long run, individuals of the same cross are more likely to get along, and to have a deeper understanding and feeling of complicity than those of the same element. In the Sagittarius and Leo example—besides sharing the passion, the energy, and a need to express themselves and to shine of the fire element, they have little else in common. They may share some common interests, but they will go about them in a completely different manner. Virgos need a good reason to do what they set out to do, while Taurus natives just need to want to do something. On a deeper level, they will have difficulty understanding each other. Although initially electrified and charmed, to a Sagittarius native the Aries may seem superficial and self-centred.

This does not imply that same-cross relationships are the only ones worth pursuing. Different-cross relationships can be very fulfilling as long as the relationship is treated with a certain degree of maturity and when basic ego needs have been met by the individuals. There remains, however, a common base in the same-cross relationship that transcends any cultural, educational, or generational boundaries. A person involved in a relationship with someone of a cross other than their own will, under stressful circumstances or periods of crisis, tend to gravitate toward someone of their own cross in search of support. This is especially likely to occur during periods of self-reevaluation or of identity crisis. Sometimes, in finding someone of the same cross, a connection is made and the person believes to have found true love. If the person is married or in a committed relationship, such an encounter can further compound the situation, since

The Crosses in the Life Experience

on top of an identity crisis, the person now has to contend with an extramarital affair. I have seen individuals return to their former mate following the disappointment of such an extramarital affair with a seemingly kindred-spirited cross, but this usually requires therapy, and much time has to be allowed for the healing of both parties to occur.

People of two different crosses may be speaking essentially the same words, but these words can have totally different meanings. The mutable person who says that he loves you may actually mean that he needs to be with you in order to feel complete and whole. The fixed person who says that he loves you may be saying that he likes you because you recognize him for who he is and don't want him to change. The cardinal person who says that she loves you may be saying that you make her feel alive and so this must be love.

In healthy relationships with couples of different crosses, there is frequently a shared-cross influence, often including the Moon, the Ascendant, or personal planets (Mercury, Venus, Mars). You may find a Pisces-Leo couple where the Pisces has a fixed Moon or Ascendant and the Leo has Mercury and Venus in Virgo. They will be able to connect on some levels, although not always in the deeply personal way that a Pisces and a Virgo couple might relate.

The same-cross relationship does not automatically guarantee the success of the relationship. The challenge of the same-cross relationship is that the individuals involved will be confronted not only with the positive aspects of their own nature but also the negative; so alike, both in positive *and* negative ways. If these negative traits are conveniently ignored or denied expression, they may never be addressed. In not being addressed, they will never be corrected. These relationships can range from the narcissistic—"He's just like me, he reflects me, this is safe and I like it"—to the confrontational, where the negative trait is mirrored back, resulting in a deadlock of will versus will (fixed), a power struggle (cardinal), or a control situation (mutable). Very often, our most vehement reactions to another person's behaviour are a result of this mirroring process. We react to what we see mirrored back to us, our own failings or what we consider to be our negative traits, or the tendencies we reject or do not approve of.

Different-cross relationships hold a natural mystique due to their basic differentness. The partner seems so attractive because he or she appears to possess the qualities of our failings. To a strongly fixed person, the energy of the cardinal person can be captivating and intriguing, while the eloquence and versatility of a mutable person can be enchanting. The other cross has qualities that we do not have. Complementarity has often been encouraged in matching individuals for a lifetime together. Overall, in seeking long-lasting compatibility in a personal relationship, a shared-cross influence will be a tremendous boon, providing a point of reference where each can connect with the other in a fundamental and familiar way.

6

Working with the Crosses

Individuals with charts that have a preponderance of one or two crosses and a lack in another will usually gravitate toward areas that favour the talents of the strong crosses. When a chart is lacking in mutable energy, for example, the person will find it difficult to work in a position where people skills and communication are essential, and so will seek work in areas such as management, if they have a strong cardinal influence, or production, with a strong fixed influence. A lack of cardinal energy will make it difficult for a person to manifest drive and leadership under all circumstances, whether easy or hard. A lack of fixed energy may result in a lack of interest in seeing a project through to completion. The more complex the job, or the greater the responsibility and power, the greater the overall skill set required to fulfil this job. This can at some point bring the individual in direct confrontation with his weaker cross. He may choose to avoid these aspects of the job, or delegate them to someone more qualified; alternatively, he may wish to take the bull by the horns and work hard at developing the missing skills.

Individuals with balanced charts, those in which the planets are evenly distributed among the crosses, will experience a broader range of personal potential and can express more than one area of interest and potential ability over a period of time. An Aries client with three cardinal planets, three mutable, and four fixed, once described how he had made his way up in a company by working in shipping and distribution (mutable), then moved up to design and production (fixed) and finished with a management position (cardinal). He effectively characterized how he had worked his way through the crosses in his chart. On the other hand, with evenly distributed cross energy, a person might have difficulty focusing in one area of expertise, unless that area requires the person to be multitalented.

A chart does not necessarily have to have a significant imbalance, such as the chart of Michael, with its nine fixed planets, in order to have a cross influence. A strategically placed configuration, such as the mutable opposition in Carol's chart, or a stellium in one of the angles, can significantly increase the importance of a cross influence. The astrologer must in a way feel his way around the chart and allow the natural disposition of the natal chart, as well as current transits and progressions, to reveal themselves in the process of interpretation.

Healing Cardinal Afflictions

The lack of cardinal energy in a chart can result in an inability to hold and maintain an ideal, difficulty projecting forward or moving ahead in life, or a lack of hope that nurtures the pursuit of these dreams. A lack of vision can prevent the individual from spreading his wings and allowing the natural process of personal expansion to occur. Without healthy ideals to nurture the spirit, there is a lack of motivation to explore avenues other than the known ones. This type of person does not know how to start, plan, undertake, or initiate situations. They may have difficulty changing track and adopting new directions in life. They will tend to downplay themselves socially, assuming a roll that is more modest than their real potential indicates. They oftentimes cannot work with long-term plans, preferring the comfort of the immediate rather than the sometimes frightful challenges of the unknown. They are likely to be reluctant to take on leadership roles, or to avoid doing so altogether.

People with little (one planet) or no cardinal energy also find it very difficult to maintain a sufficient degree of hopefulness, so that during trying times, it is difficult for them to imagine that things will eventually work themselves out. To these individuals, the future remains an intangible abstraction or something that is beyond the realm of immediate control. Note that a lack of planets in cardinal signs implies a substantial distribution of planets in the fixed and/or mutable signs. Fixed signs generally do not deal well in abstractions and mutables need to have control.

A Sagittarius client with Mercury, the Moon, Uranus, Pluto, and Mars in mutable signs, and with no planets in cardinal signs, laughed knowingly when I explained what was meant by the lack of cardinal energy in her chart. "You mean planning?" And she shook her head, indicating clearly that one of the most difficult things for her was to make a plan, and that it was even more difficult for her to stick to it. She was highly intelligent, versatile, an excellent organizer, and had been a successful career woman, but now that it was time for her to get in touch with her inner dream so that she could establish a new ideal for herself and modify her life direction so that it would better reflect her inner soul, she was at a loss. At this time in her life, when it was necessary for her to plant a new beacon to follow, this normally dynamic, capable, and confident woman felt uncertain of her path, unsure that she could walk into an unknown future and be able to manage as successfully as she had in the past. Despite years of successful life experience, in the face of an unknown future, faith and confidence failed her.

In order to counter this lack of cardinal energy, the person will need to define some short-term, very attainable goals, as a way of building confidence in her ability to successfully plan for the future. Once the short-term goals are accomplished, then appropriate mid-term goals can be defined, and the process would continue until a more long-term plan has been established.

An excess of cardinal energy, by the structural nature of the crosses, implies the existence of squares and oppositions, indicating much energy and a potential for inner stresses and challenges. If improperly harnessed, this concentration of cardinal energy can manifest as an impulse to act without concern for the value of the outcome (little or no fixed energy), to act for the thrill of the action (abundance of cardinal energy), and to act for no apparent reason (little or no mutable energy). In these cases, passion can get in the way of practical reality. A lack of sense of self can lead to a tendency to seek stimulus and direction from others, or to seek out an external cause, especially if the person does not believe in the value of his own worth. An excess of cardinal energy can also cause a person to pursue goals that are completely unattainable and unrealistic; in fact, to lose touch with reality. They can become delusional about their personal power and even abusive in the expression of the excessive energy.

The inability to direct the flow of energy in a healthy and constructive activity can result in energy being wasted through anything from excessive fantasizing to actions that lack reason, purpose, or direction, performed solely as a vehicle to vent pent-up energy. Thoughtless, daring childhood pranks and thrill-seeking acts, are also good examples of misdirected cardinal energy. Adolescents and young adults that can't get enough partying are a typical example of the need for manifestation of this energy. All-night raves are typical cardinal haunts. Improperly channelled cardinal energy can, in worst-case scenarios, erupt into acts of verbal and emotional abuse or even physical violence, often directed at those closest at hand. In consultation work, whenever possible, a regimen of sports and physical activity can be recommended as a way of helping the imbalanced cardinal individual return to a state of inner equilibrium. Once a more peaceful state has been established, the person can then begin to define new personal or professional goals, or to establish a new life purpose, one that best reflects current and personal needs. As cardinal energies are directed toward a more productive end, the healing process can begin. The key element in the cardinal individual's search for fulfillment and personal success is the need to identify and then to progress toward a goal, or an ideal of personal significance.

A personal trainer with the Sun in Cancer square Uranus in Libra, a very energetic and highly strung young woman, admitted self-consciously during a consultation that she just loved to party. Then she asked if it was okay to be so much into partying, specifying that she was almost addicted to all-night raves, and wondering if it was a bad thing, or if she was a bad person because of it. The cardinal part of her chart was asking a person in a position of authority, in this case the astrologer, for permission or for her blessing to participate in an activity that gave her much pleasure and probably also allowed free expression of her boundless energy. The strong mutable showing, in particular Saturn (authority) conjunct Venus (values), wanted to know if this was bad behaviour on her part, a typical mutable concern. Her physical body took the brunt of this manifestation of energy, indicated by her elevated Moon in Taurus. In this case, there was a definite need for an appropriate outlet of expression of energy. This could have been managed in various ways; for example, through creative dance, sports, or physical training, activities that would prove to have less wear and tear on the body in the long-term and that might allow her to further develop her skills in the process.

The cardinal signs will be inclined to benefit from forms of meditation or personal development that touch the emotions, or from forms that propose personal challenges to self-control, to personal power, such as for example the way of the warrior or self-mastery, or approaches that challenge physical, mental, and emotional barriers. Cardinal-sign individuals respond to strong leaders, and strong leadership. They need to be kept active. They also need to be involved in projects that are within the realm of the possible, and so it may be necessary for cardinal person to tailor expectations to more feasible goals. The ability to visualize a dream, to dream of a better future, to take risks and reach out and embrace change and new experiences is found in the cardinal planets in one's chart. Cardinal blockages will prevent a person from being able to see into the future, to imagine a better life and to act on these mental images.

One day, I recommended to a very active cardinal client that she might benefit by setting some time aside for herself for quiet, relaxing activities, such as a hot bubble bath now and then. She exclaimed that she would love a hot bath, but she felt it was such a passive, nonproductive activity. Knowing the cardinal sign's inclination for movement, I suggested something I discovered to appease my own cardinal planets: fill the bath only half full with hot water using your favourite essential oils or bubble bath; climb in and let the water continue to fill the bath in a slow easy trickle. That way, you will have the sense of movement with the water running, and a constantly hot bath for your soaking and relaxing enjoyment.

Rina's chart shows a very strong mutable influence, six planets including the Ascendant ruler and the Ascendant, and a healthy fixed showing with three planets and the Midheaven, including the Midheaven ruler. Despite a shortage of cardinal energy, Rina has not been prevented from achieving a certain degree of professional success. She has made excellent use of her mutable energy by acquiring and mastering unique technical skills (Uranus with Pluto and Mercury in Virgo) in the communications-related (mutable) field of custom sign design. From her home workshop, she produces posters, banners, signs, and lettering for a broad variety of applications, from storefront signs to lettering on vehicles.

Rina thoroughly enjoys her work. She has a friendly and talkative disposition and is very pleasant to work with. She has admitted to being most comfortable when she is in control of her life (mutable). There have been few radical changes in the course

Working with the Crosses

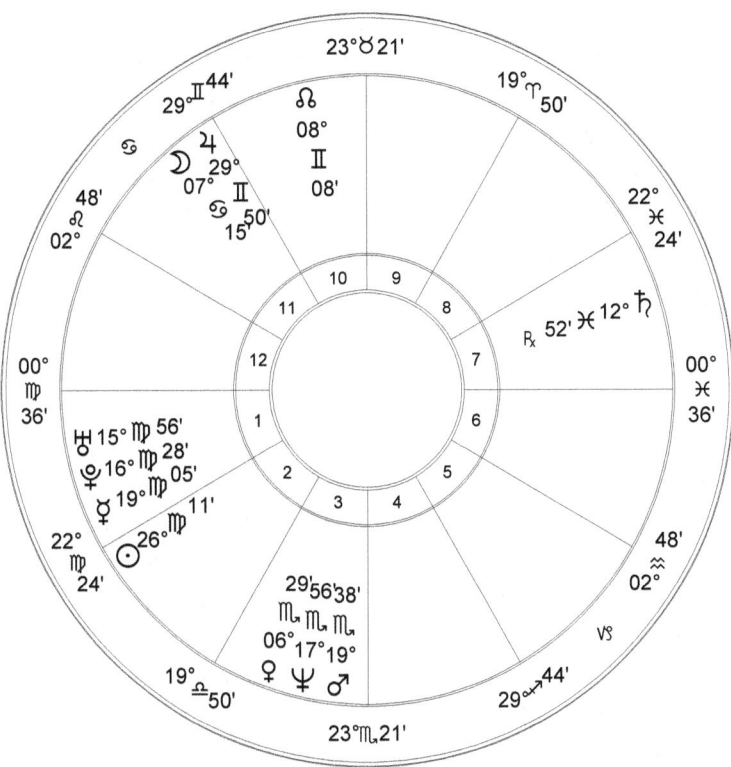

Rina

of her life, contrary to popular teaching regarding the mutable signs, as she prefers to deal with situations which she can manage by the use of her skills, wit, and abilities. With this approach, her company has made slow but steady and risk-free progress.

Rina takes things one day at a time, or rather, one crisis at a time, and does not worry too far in advance about what might or might not happen. This is not to say that she does not worry; quite the contrary. Like any good Virgo, she expends inordinate amounts of energy fussing and worrying about day-to-day matters. Once she has finished worrying, there is little energy or inclination remaining to consider cardinal issues: long-term planning, goal-setting, exploring dreams, or examining expectations. The mutable-fixed combination focuses on getting things done (fixed) as they were meant to be done (mutable), and seeing that the customer is pleased with the result (mutable), and that she is paid for a job well done (fixed). Naturally, she has tremendous patience for the painstaking nature of her work (Virgo), and she also exercises great care in providing the best quality possible in materials and workmanship.

When Rina came to see me, she had been through a relatively smooth growth phase and was about to enter a challenging period of transits where she would have to make decisions about the direction of her business, and about how large she wanted it to grow and at what rate. I asked her if she had established a budget for her business and made a three-year plan. She had not. The thought alone made her shudder. To think of the future, to consider such abstractions as long-term planning, to move away from the comfort of her known sphere of control, was a challenge she was not equipped to deal with. This did not mean that Rina's business would never grow because she did not have a business plan. But in order to manage her company's progress effectively, she might need to call on some outside help, someone with a little cardinal business-management sense. Without any cardinal energy, it remains difficult for Rina to establish and be motivated by long-term goals. Planning (cardinal) does not provide the rewards that dealing with immediate problems and situations (mutable and fixed) does.

Sensitizing Rina to this discrepancy in her chart was not a difficult task. Being quick, clever, and very bright, she recognized right away the need to compensate for her low cardinal energy. You will notice the Cancer Moon trine Pisces Saturn; this particular aspect has strengthened her need to provide for long-term material and emotional security, which she has attended to with quiet, steady effort. Where she will find more difficulty is in the conceptualization of possibilities for her company. Venus, Neptune and Mars in Scorpio in the third house give her a strong creative and artistic base. She has dabbled with various art forms, including painting, and has actually been struggling with ideas for a painting for some years now. Here the lack of cardinal energy will make it difficult for her to move from known, technical, mechanical forms (mutable) toward inspired (note also a lack of fire), visionary, imaginative (cardinal) creations. Any creative, artistic productions will have to be guided and sustained by a purely intuitive, creative process (nine yin planets). This will require that she trust her perceptions (fixed) and allow herself to express what lies deep within her spirit, a challenging path for the need-to-be-in-control mutable!

Healing Fixed Afflictions

A lack of fixed energy in a chart can indicate a lack of realism, or an inability, sometimes even an unwillingness, to see things as they are. This can also indicate a difficulty achieving concrete results or bringing ideals or ideas to fruition. This leads to a lack of feeling of satisfaction and difficulty attaining the self-validation that is the natural consequence of personal accomplishment. Hence, there can be a delay in the development of a healthy sense of self, or identity. These individuals will seek to justify their behaviour and their decisional processes by using criteria that are either external to themselves (mutable) or that are based on an ideal or cause (cardinal), depending on the surrounding parental and environmental influences. This type will rarely say that they have chosen to do such and such simply because they feel like it, or that this is what they enjoy doing, unless they are taught to do so. This would be deemed very self-indulgent; while for fixed-sign individuals, this is a very important criteria for determining whether or not they are on the right track.

A young woman, a Gemini with seven cardinal planets and mutable angles, with no fixed points in her chart, came for a consultation at a time when she was very confused about her general life orientation. She had worked as a model (an archetypal Gemini occupation) and had experienced a certain degree of success in this area, but felt dissatisfied with herself and with her life in general. She was not sure that this was the "right way to go" (mutable analysis), uncertain that this route would, in the long run, give her the inner satisfaction she sought. Anyone on the outside would immediately think that this beautiful young woman had it all: beauty, youth, an exciting career, hobnobbing with the rich and famous. In fact, she was torn between a desire to find a life that would provide inner fulfillment and her attraction for the "fame and glory" (her own words) of the world of high-fashion modelling and hanging out with the rich and beautiful people of Hollywood.

The absence of fixed planets in her chart indicates a difficulty in linking up with her true identity. She wanted to know whether or not she would be famous (the mutable planets seeking the guarantees, the cardinal ones seeking the acclamation). Without a true sense of personal identity, she seeks approval through her looks, and since she does not believe that she is beautiful, all the applause she seeks and receives will never satisfy her inner self. Her real need is to know who she is and that she is truly beautiful on the inside. She needs to develop a sense of self-worth (fixed); something that no amount of applause or fame will satisfy. This imbalance indicates a life path that requires attention to the development of a true sense of inner self.

WORKING WITH THE CROSSES

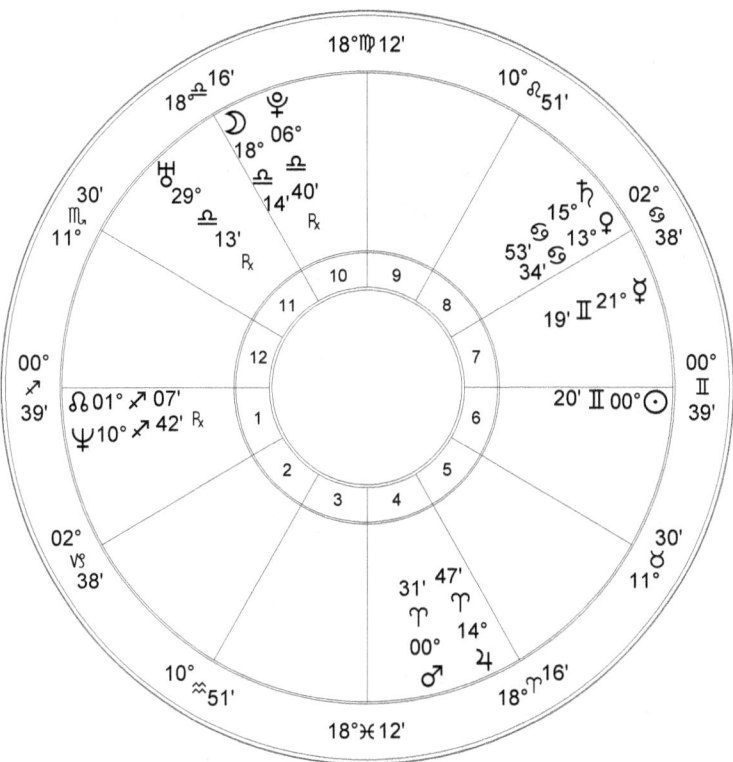

Model

An excess of fixed energy will indicate individuals who are potentially very creative and productive, but who can be immovable and can tend to cocoon about their own interests. Michael is a composer of classical music. Creative by nature and entirely fixed (nine fixed planets), he lives mostly from desire. He enjoys the company of like-minded friends, loves to talk and express his views, and enjoys the good life, good food, and a good movie. Highly talented, educated, and intelligent, he lives for his compositions, which he works and reworks over and over again. One of his biggest fears is that one day, he will have his day and his music will be played, but afterward there is a chance that it will not be well reviewed by the critics. For Michael, this is a very real fear, one which might keep him concentrated on his works, rather than on other aspects of the business of music, such as marketing (cardinal) and networking (mutable). With a lack of mutable energy in his chart, he will not go out of his way to create the ties with those who might have an impact on his musical career—they should come to him, he is, after all, the creator; with a lack of cardinal energy, he does not manifest his worldly ambitions.

Strong fixed-sign individuals tend to be opinionated and can be narrow-minded. They may find it very difficult to adapt to changing realities and will hold on to the old much longer than is necessary or even healthy. They may also refuse to accept alternate realities and can express bigotry and profound hatred toward ideas, lifestyles, philosophies, or cultures that are different from their own. They tend to hold on to the old and known reality rather than move forward to discover new realities. They can lack imagination, be unable to visualize new possibilities, and avoid looking ahead. They can tend to self-destructive behaviour when they become trapped in long-standing negative and unproductive phases. Fixed energy at its worst is replete with hatred and can be very destructive. It is absolute and knows no compromises. Fixed individuals can be entirely selfish and completely intolerant of realities that do not fit into their own paradigm of reality.

Working with the Crosses

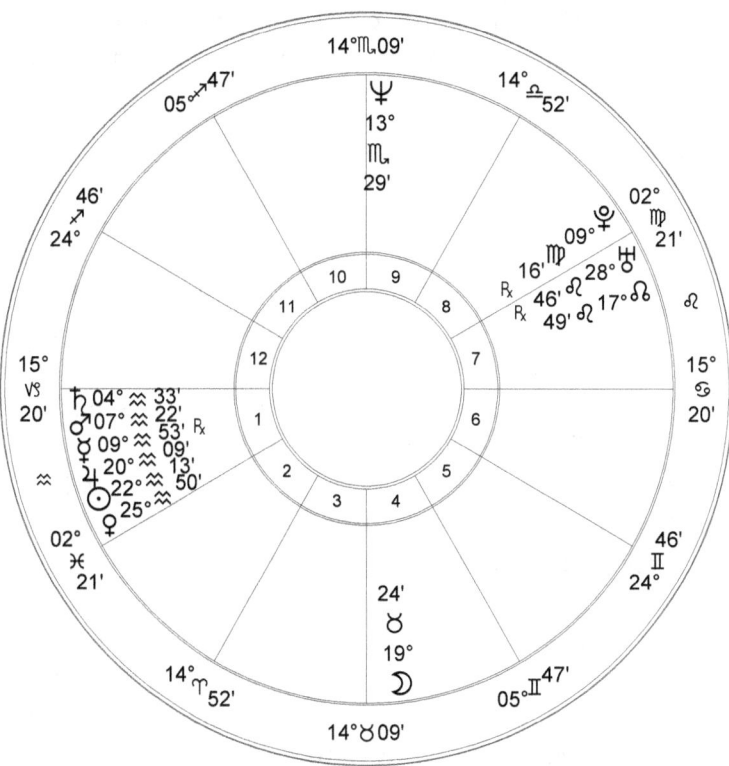

Michael

During periods of intense activation, such as during times of challenging transits and progressions to fixed points in a natal chart, a person can be inclined to withdraw into a self-imposed cocoon, much as a tender caterpillar will do in order to create the environment that will enable its transformation from one level of being to the next. It is usually a delicate and subjective process, one in which the person finds himself to be vulnerable to external confrontations, where self-protection through some degree of isolation is necessary. A fixed process can indeed be a solitary one, and individuals in such a state need not only the acceptance of those near and dear to them, but also as much free space as possible in which to "find themselves."

Meditations that centre on gratitude, or on thanking the universe for its bounty, can be very helpful forms of exercise for fixed signs or persons experiencing fixed-sign difficulties. Reflections on the positive attributes of self, on one's qualities and aptitudes, can help reinforce a more healthy perception of self, facilitating the inner healing process. Fixed signs may have a bit of difficulty with the self-help tools that require extensive use of imagination and visualization; they will be more comfortable with a more personal and concrete approach. Impeccability in action would also be a good tool for fixed signs, requiring that the person be 100 percent present in the act, fully present in thought, action, heart, and movement. A reading of a simple yet highly inspiring story, such as *The Alchemist* by Paulo Coelho, or even *Jonathan Livingston Seagull* by Richard Bach, might help stimulate the dream function when fixed-sign individuals find themselves stuck in a rut.

Healing Mutable Afflictions

The lack of mutable energy in a chart can cause a person to feel unintelligent, or to feel as though they have a learning handicap. This does not mean that a lack of mutable signs indicates an actual lack of intelligence; it means that the native must find other means besides the normal mutable routes, such as language and speech, to express themselves and to acquire knowledge. In some ways, these individuals will compensate by developing a type of practical intelligence that is most effective in dealing with their particular life situations and in achieving personal success, but which may be somewhat less effective in more academic fields. The person with a lack of mutable can sit in on a class for hours on end, read books, listen to lectures, but somehow the information just does not sink in. They find it difficult to retain information for its own sake, unless this information is acquired in the course of researching a subject of personal interest, in which case, the information is more readily integrated (often found with a strong fixed-sign chart), or when studying a subject that nurtures ideals and goals (a strong cardinal chart). With a lack of mutable energy, there is difficulty making new information connect with old, and so expansion of the body of knowledge takes more time. A person with a lack of mutable energy will learn more readily in a hands-on setting, where direct experience and perception will help establish the knowledge in memory by making it personalized. A lack of mutable energy can also lead to a difficulty in trusting others or trusting knowledge that comes from others. They will need to try things for themselves; these are the true doubting Thomases.

An excess of mutable energy can cause the person to lose a sense of self, to become wrapped in the affairs of others, and to seek acceptance and approval from others. A client with the Sun, Moon, Saturn, and Mercury in mutable Virgo, and five cardinal planets (leaving only one fixed planet, that being Pluto in Leo), who was keeping herself very busy helping family members and friends solve their problems (seven of her planets are in the seventh and eighth houses) on top of being engaged in an already demanding career, was wondering why she remained dissatisfied with her life, despite being so busy and involved. She admitted to feeling validated through her need to be needed by others (Virgo, mutable), but at the same time was pulled by a desire to do something for herself, something that would be personally validating, actions that may not be directly attached to the needs of others. Although self-aware, bright, articulate, and rather honest about herself, she lacks a healthy dose of self-*ishness* (low fixed energy), the impulse to validate self for the sake of self. She needs to learn that it is okay to think of herself, that by becoming stronger in her sense of self, she will have more to give to others.

The natal chart is a complex map and there are many ways of approaching its interpretation. In consultation, clients will oftentimes openly take the lead and direct the interpretation of the chart and its transits into areas of personal interest. At the same time that interpretations are led by clients into directions of personal interest, they are also veered from areas which they would prefer to avoid or even deny altogether. This, by the way, tends to happen more readily with mutable charts. As mutables are relational and tend to take control of circumstances when they can, this is easy to understand. These are the clients who say, when they return for an update, "I listened to the tape and all I could hear was the sound of my own voice! Please, don't let me talk so much this time." However, as talking is part of their nature, try as they might, they lay their voice once again onto tape.

In the example that follows, the client contributed to the orientation of the consultation to a large extent. This same example also illustrates how a planetary configuration or focal point can have a significant impact, even if it is found in a cross other than the native's Sun sign cross; in this case the mutable-sign oppositions in the chart of a cardinal native. In other words, one does not have to be a mutable sign in order to suffer a mutable affliction. The challenging aspect or planetary placement will act as a sore point in the person's life when not effectively directed into a positive form of expression.

When Carol came to me looking for guidance, she had been in a process of reevaluating her life orientation. Clearly, the strong air element in the chart indicates a talkative disposition, with the emphasis on Libra giving a strong inclination toward social interaction and the sharing of experiences with others. Knowing that the consultation would soon turn to the question "But do you see a relationship in the chart?" I started by humorously bringing up the importance of relationships and that this was likely to be an important issue in the consultation. This immediately brought a smile to the client, who graciously refrained from pursuing this question, at least for the first half of the consultation. The more interesting part of the chart came into focus as I began to explore character traits, possible career orientation and personal orientation.

Although Carol did not immediately inquire about her love life, all the comments she made as I interpreted the chart were in relation to other persons or external circumstances, such as mother, mentor, death of father, boyfriend, purchase of a condo, etc. The general purpose of the comments was clearly to justify the choices and decisions she had made throughout her life. These responses can be attributed, in large part, to the mutable oppositions that cross the chart horizontally, acting as a barrier, keeping Mars, the planet of action, isolated from the rest of the chart. The mutable barrier seemed to keep her energy tied up in the mind, and in this case, with Uranus, Pluto, and Jupiter involved, the mind proved to be a very capable and powerful aspect of her nature.

There were two main problems to be considered at this time with this chart: on the one hand, the strong emphasis of the Libra self/other axis, and on the other hand, the tendency toward projection of the mutable oppositions. The Libra aspect will weigh the options and attempt to balance the power, while the mutable energy will try to identify with "the right thing to do." The relational bent of the chart will likely lead to an inner dialogue that goes as follows: "It's because I didn't get any support from my mother… The condo ties me down…, I can't (…) because…"

Carol's next line of questioning referred to her future choices: If she did choose to move forward in the direction of her natural inclinations, could I tell her, from the chart, whether or not she would be successful and whether or not she would find a suitable life partner? In other words, the mutable (relational cross) opposition (relational aspect) wanted to know whether or not it was worth the effort to make a change at this point in her life, and could I give her any guarantees that she would be successful in her efforts? In this type of situation, the person will find balance and ultimately satisfaction when she has turned her energy inward, when the struggle for success becomes internalized and is no longer projected externally. In other words, when she assumes responsibility for herself, she will be free to move forward. Several months later, Carol did decide to move forward and actually found a very satisfactory job, one that was much more in keeping with her talents and abilities.

As previously pointed out, mutable afflictions in the natal chart can cause a person to become trapped in an endless cycle of justification and rationalization. In fact, mutables can analyze until they become paralyzed, a common ailment among members of this cross. This paralysis leads to procrastination, indecision and inaction. In such cases, one can suspect the source of the paralysis or the payoff for inaction to be fear of accepting the consequences of one's actions, fear of retribution if the result is in some way wrong, or a refusal to accept responsibility, such as in a Peter Pan Syndrome. Such a situation leads to tremendous inner stress, anxiety and feelings of inadequacy, and lack of personal fulfillment. The only way to break this cycle is for the individual to decide upon a course of action and to be willing to accept the consequences, no matter the outcome, of this action. A simplified course of action may be chosen at first, so that the person can become accustomed to this new process. When a sufficient level of confidence has been attained, a more difficult decision can be approached.

Another consideration for the mutable signs is "What will others think?" To this concern, there is but a simple answer: People generally don't give a damn much about what other people

WORKING WITH THE CROSSES

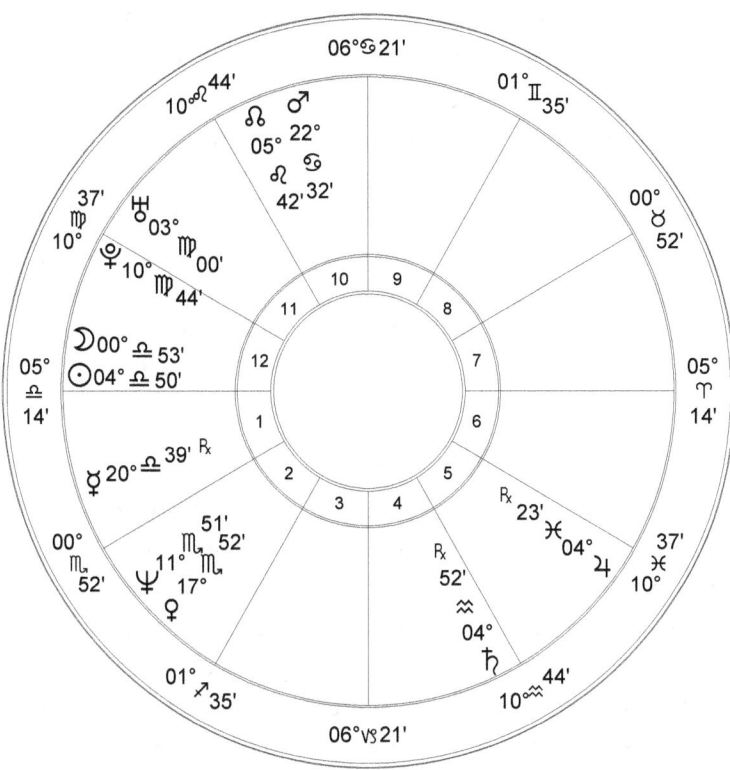

Carol

do. This can become another convenient excuse for postponing important decisions and actions. An excellent source of insight for persons who find themselves trapped in an endless loop of rational paralysis is the popular book by Virgo native Dr. Phil McGraw *Life Strategies*. His approach is truly no nonsense and down to earth and does not allow for endless mental meanderings. His life law number one is, "You either get it, or you don't," which does not leave much room for getting lost in the never-ending process of rationalization in which individuals marked by the mutable signs often find themselves trapped.

Working with Keywords

For the beginning student, given the large number of factors to be considered, the interpretation of an astrology chart can appear daunting. To further complicate matters, no two charts are identical, and each must be interpreted in the context of the life of the individual. In working with astrology and numerology, I have found that, oftentimes, the quickest and simplest way to arrive at a clear and relevant interpretation of a pattern or transit is with the use of keywords. With just a couple of relevant and applicable key principles, it becomes easy to identify what is going on in the person's life and also what would be the most appropriate course of action. As you become familiar with the nature of the crosses, feel free to add words, images, and phrases that speak to you. The following keywords were adapted from *L'Hermès: Dictionnaire des correspondances symboliques* by Marc Bériault, Pauline Edward, and Axel Harvey.

The Cardinal Cross
authority, initiative, planning, the challenge

BASIC PRINCIPLE
Truth: equating the idea to reality; the idea becomes reality, or reality must become the idea. The authority principle, to initiate the idea, plan, concept, code; submission to the idea, etc. or to whoever represents it.

GENERAL
Impulse, ideal, audacity, ambition, principles, making the abstract into reality through action; great need for a sense of purpose; the power of authority.

PSYCHOLOGICAL
The big question is in the source of the idea, the plan, etc. May act without thinking or without concern for the value of things; problems of validation, or identity can lend a tendency to give authority to an idea, concept, or code (or person incarnating these) that is exterior to one's self. Negative manifestation: seeks sensation of power, authority, or self-importance. Delusional, tendency to self-glorification or self-aggrandizement. Will confront authority figures in order to test their power. When feelings of inadequacy exist, will level the playing field with whatever means work. Would rather suffer than not feel anything at all.

MENTAL
Polarizes attention on the plan; conceptualization; structured mind.

TALENTS
The entrepreneur; turning ideas into actions; planning, forward movement; applied mathematics; execution; equations; leadership and motivation; contributes through drive, ambition and conviction.

CAREERS
Executives of all types; builder, construction, foreman, officer, engineer, politician, orchestra conductor, sales, management and leadership positions; positions of authority; motivational speakers and coaches.

The Fixed Cross
creation, reality, perception, the result

BASIC PRINCIPLE
Beauty; reality as a manifestation of what is (being, essence). Identity: I as an intangible which takes form by manifesting itself creatively; hence "I" becomes aware. Value: as the fact of expressing what is (reality) or its consequence—the product, or the result.

GENERAL
Accomplishment; processes (concept in movement); will, realization, passion, perseverance, autonomy; the bottom line; the body, sensations, definitions of reality, direct experience.

PSYCHOLOGICAL
Will not accept that something cannot work; feelings of powerlessness lead to inaction, followed by partial or total self-destruction; identity problems lead to the realization of the concepts of others. Validation: the fact of perceiving and accepting the value of what is without the need for justification. Negative manifestation: difficulty imagining or accepting a reality other than one's own, thus creating immobility or inflexibility in the life; stubbornness, narrow-mindedness; retrograde attitude; stuck in the mud; difficulty accepting change. Tendency to flog a dead horse; will not let go.

MENTAL
Concentration, intuition; finds the solution before the explanation; perception as a tool for evaluation.

TALENTS

Getting the job done; realization, accomplishment, invention, doing, problem-solving; results-oriented; determining worth and value; identifying what is important.

CAREERS

Production, creativity, management (related to production) and management of resources, artists, banking, commerce; can work independently, with little or no supervision.

The Mutable Cross
communication, relating, projection, the word

BASIC PRINCIPLE

Good-bad; science; the model of known reality, whether desired or not; conformity of the model (scientific, moral, religious, etc.) to reality. Communication, to diffuse or exchange knowledge and information about life; techniques, how-to. Excommunication, or, the exclusion of that which does not conform to the model (whether self-imposed or externally imposed).

GENERAL

Scientific or philosophical thought; reflection, adaptation and flexibility; intelligence; models, symbols, language, information; exchanges and interactions of all types. Control and manipulation of people, things, data, situations. Knowledge as a symbolic representation of reality, which requires to be verified through testing.

PSYCHOLOGICAL

Feeling of powerlessness leads to identification with a model at the expense of individuality. Validation problems lead to acting out or playing out the role that is validated, or to isolation in non communication. Justification, rationalization. Negative manifestation: lack of participation, sterile analysis; loss of touch with reality due to a lack of validation through tests and direct experience. Distrust of self and others; projection; use of guilt to manipulate others.

MENTAL
Great capacity for thinking, deduction, analysis, study, evaluation, classification, and validation of data and information; difficulty synthesizing.

TALENTS
Communications; science; anything related to analysis and knowledge; to train, teach, form or shape; care-giving and support.

CAREERS
Communications, sales, intermediaries, technicians, writers, customer service, entertainment, education, spokespersons, researchers, social sciences, health and welfare-related careers.

Bibliography & Resources

Andrews, Robert. *The Columbia Dictionary of Quotations*. New York: Columbia University Press, 1993.

Arroyo, Stephen, M.A. *Astrology, Psychology and the Four Elements*. Davis, CA: CRCS Publications, 1975.

Bériault, Marc, Edward, Pauline and Harvey, Axel. *L'Hermès, Dictionnaire des correspondances symboliques*. Outremont, Quebec: Collection Aurélia, Bxx éditeur, 1993.

deVore, Nicholas. *Encyclopedia of Astrology*. 1947. Reprint, Brampton, Ontario: Ballantrae, 1986.

Hirsig, Werner. *Manuel D'Astrologie*. Montreal, Québec: Presses Select Ltée, 1970.

Hone, Margaret. *The Modern Textbook of Astrology*. London: L.N. Fowler & Co. Ltd., 1972.

Jones, Marc Edmund. *Astrology: How and Why it Works*. 1945. Reprint, Santa Fe, NM: Aurora Press, Inc.

Kelly, Susan. "Directions." January, 1988. A newsletter for members of the former F.C.A. (Federation of Canadian Astrologers).

March, Marion D., & Joan McEvers. *The Only Way to Learn Astrology, Volume I: Basic Principles*. San Diego, CA: ACS Publications, Inc., 1976.

Martin Luther King, Jr: The Peaceful Warrior, NY: Pocket Books, 1968.

McGraw, Phillip C. *Life Strategies: Doing What Works, Doing What Matters*. New York: Hyperion Books, 1999.

The New Book of Knowledge. Danbury, CT: Grolier, Inc., 1988.

The New Lexicon Webster's Encyclopedic Dictionary of the English Language. Canadian Edition. New York: Lexicon Publications, Inc., 1988.

Oken, Alan. *Alan Oken's Complete Astrology*. New York: Bantam Books, 1981.

Time-Life Books, eds. *The European Emergence, TimeFrame A.D. 1500–1600*. Alexandria, VA: Time-Life Books, 1989.

Horoscope Sources

Harvey, Martin. "Elizabeth of England and Three Men." *The Astrological Journal* xviii 1 (winter 1975-1976):10-19.
   Queen Elizabeth I

The Blackwell Collection
Blackwell, A.H., compiler. The Historical Data Collection (software database in Nova, Solar Fire or compatible chart formats). Astrolabe, Inc. 1989; P.O. Box 1750, Brewster, MA.; www.alabe.com.
   Henry Ford

Lois Rodden's AstroDatabank
www.astrodatabank.com
   Bill Gates
   Dr. Martin Luther King, Jr.
   Marc Edmund Jones
   Oprah Winfrey
   Steve Jobs

Matrix Celebrity Astro Search
www.thenewage.com
   W. Somerset Maugham
   Charlotte Brontë

The Zodiacal Zephyr
http://miva.zodiacal.com/hunt.mv
   Mother Teresa

About the Author

Pauline Edward is an astrologer-numerologist, speaker, Certified Professional Coach and Group Leader. She is the recipient of a Chamber of Commerce Accolades Award for excellence in business practice. With a background in the sciences and a fascination for all things mystical, Pauline's journey has been enriched by a wide range of experiences from research in international economics, technical writing in R&D and computer training, to studies in astrology, numerology, meditation, yoga, spirituality, shamanism, the Bach Flower Remedies, herbology, healing and reiki. Her profound desire to uncover the truth about the meaning of life was the inspiration behind her lifetime of writing.

Pauline is available for speaking engagements and workshops. For information about upcoming events and publications, visit her website: http://www.paulineedward.com.

Aquarius
The Age of Revelation, Choice and Transformation
Pauline Edward
Desert Lily Publications

This unique work by author, Astrologer-Numerologist Pauline Edward sets the journey of awakening of humanity against the backdrop of the transition from the Age of Pisces to the Age of Aquarius, a most important period of change for humanity. It explores some of the core themes found in newly emerging teachings as they relate to the current shift in consciousness. The journey of humanity over the past three Ages, Taurus, Aries and Pisces, has established the foundation of the current human condition, a condition that many are beginning to question. So it is that during this time of great shift, we have the opportunity to examine our past, where we now stand and begin to release the old and make way for significant change for all living beings as well as for our beloved planet Earth.

"Pauline's latest book clarifies our Oneness in an easy and understandable way, and is spot-on for our times in the 2020s when the healing of humanity and being IN love can bring us to the level of our awakening."
—Elizabeth Luik.

"Pauline has so effectively, as only she can, in a clear, concise and simplified manner, without all the jargon, managed to marry two subject matters that are considered by many as too complex and difficult to grasp."
—Helena Basso

"There is much here for your own growth and healing, from self-love to tapping into the Higher Self to the releasing of judgment. An inspiring work to read and reread."
—Michael J. Miller

Making Peace with God
The Journey of a *Course in Miracles* Student
Pauline Edward
Desert Lily Publications

It is said, "Seek and you will find." But what happens when your quest for the truth about life, God and the meaning of existence repeatedly fails to offer satisfactory answers? Determined to uncover the truth, you persist, and, lo and behold, you find. But what if the truth you discover challenges each and every one of your beliefs? This is the story of one woman's lifelong search for a fulfilling spirituality, one that answers the unanswerable, that is truly universal and all-inclusive and, above all, that is logical and practicable. *Making Peace with God* recounts a journey that begins with Roman Catholicism, explores various ancient and contemporary spiritualities and culminates with the extraordinary thought system of *A Course in Miracles*.

—Gary Renard, best-selling author of *The Disappearance of the Universe* highly recommends this wonderful book.

"A must read for *A Course in Miracles* students or anyone curious about its profound, mind-healing message."
—Susan Dugan, author of *Extraordinary Ordinary Forgiveness*

"*Making Peace with God* is the ultimate destination of all spiritual journeys… a story sure to save much time for the spiritual seeker."
—Alexander Marchand, author and artist of *The Universe Is a Dream: The Secrets of Existence Revealed*

"An inspiring and enjoyable book which will encourage others on their spiritual journey."
—Michael Dawson, author of *Healing the Cause*

Leaving the Desert
Embracing the Simplicity of *A Course in Miracles*
Pauline Edward
Desert Lily Publications

After completing a first reading of *A Course in Miracles*, the most challenging read of her life, the author exclaimed, "Never again!" Yet, she knew that if she were to make real progress with her life-long spiritual quest, she would need a thorough understanding of the Course's unique thought system. So, back to school she went—the school of life, that is. Though a seasoned seeker, never did she anticipate the dark nights she would encounter along the journey, nor the gift of grace that would pull her through. Readers will delight in the same profound spiritual insight, candour, humour and lively writing style as found in *Making Peace with God*.

"*Leaving the Desert: Embracing the Simplicity of A Course in Miracles*, is one of the most practical spiritual books ever written. I was struck by Pauline's ability to clearly and simply state the principles of the Course, from the beginning of her journey, through a genuine spiritual search, to her discovery of a new direction, to the understanding of miracles, and ultimately to the miracle of forgiveness in undoing the deviousness of the ego. I highly recommend this book to anyone who is on a spiritual path, and especially to those who want to get on the fast track."
—Gary Renard, Author of *The Disappearance of the Universe*

"I thoroughly enjoyed *Leaving the Desert* by Pauline Edward. It is an excellent description of the basic metaphysics and psychology of *A Course in Miracles* and its practical application in daily life, written in a clear conversational style."
—Jon Mundy, Ph.D., author of *Living A Course in Miracles*

"*In Leaving the Desert: Embracing the Simplicity of A Course in Miracles*, Pauline Edward shares her intimate quest both to fully comprehend the Course's fundamental principles despite the

ego's formidable resistance and to apply its unique forgiveness in her daily life. *Leaving the Desert* will inspire Course newbies and veterans alike with its profound, comprehensive understanding and specific examples fearlessly and generously drawn from the classroom of the author's life."
—Susan Dugan, author of *Extraordinary Ordinary Forgiveness*

"Written with humor and courageous self-disclosure, Pauline Edward's *Leaving the Desert* is a delight. Through sharing her own exploration—her commitment and her doubts—she addresses all the major topics covered in A Course in Miracles with precision and clarity. For new students as well as veterans of the Course, her overview of its purpose and methodology is excellent. Her adroit sprinkling of personal anecdotes enlivens and clarifies her path (and ours) and her honesty allows the book to be a comforting companion to those seeking to engage more artfully with this life-changing practice. You will read this book with a smile of recognition and gratitude."
—Carol Howe, author of *Never Forget To Laugh: Personal Recollections of Bill Thetford, Co-scribe of A Course in Miracles,*

"Pauline Edward delivers the concepts of *A Course in Miracles* elegantly and uncompromisingly, and with an undeniably gifted style. This book is wonderful. It offers a deep and much-needed exploration of the core message of *A Course in Miracles*. It comes from profound guidance, and places the reader at the altar of Truth. *Leaving the Desert* is a must-read for any student of the Course, or any person seeking enlightenment, who would leave no stone unturned in an endeavour to return Home to our natural state of Love."
—Robyn Busfield, author of *Forgiveness is the Home of Miracles*

Choosing the Miracle
Pauline Edward
Desert Lily Publications

This book was nearly three quarters of the way finished when, seven years into her work with *A Course in Miracles*, the author hit a wall. Although it appeared as a very high wall that would take a very long time and a whole lot of effort to be climbed, as it turned out, it simply needed to be risen above and left behind. This passing hurdle resulted in the crumbling of a lifetime of learning and a major shift in perception, the ideal condition for a true experience of the miracle. Written with the same candour, sincerity, wit and courage, this book picks up where *Leaving the Desert* left off and will be an inspiration for all spiritual seekers.

"The greatest compliment an author of a spiritual book can receive is that their extension of love is felt throughout the book. I found that *Choosing the Miracle* not only inspired me, but gave me a direct experience of God."
—Reverend Dan Costello

"In *Choosing the Miracle* Pauline Edward graciously plants yet another shimmering guidepost for her fellow Course students. By sharing the entertaining insights gleaned from her own ongoing growth with *A Course in Miracles*, Pauline Edward looks through the ceaseless lies of the ego to reveal the truth of spirit. Stay on Course by Choosing the Miracle."
—Alexander Marchand, author of *The Universe Is a Dream*

"*Choosing the Miracle* is a wonderful account of the simplicity of actually "living" *A Course in Miracles*, and opens the door for dedicated students who are WILLING to live and walk the Truth right here, right now, TODAY!"
—Robyn Busfield, author of *Forgiveness is the Home of Miracles*

The Power of Time
Understanding the Cycles of Your Life's Path
Pauline Edward
Llewellyn Worldwide

Don't wait around for life to just "happen." Develop a solid, successful life plan with guidance from astrologer-numerologist Pauline Edward. Whether your goals are personal or professional, *The Power of Time* will help you take advantage of the powerful natural cycles at work in your life. Simple calculations based on numerology reveal where you are in each nine-year cycle and what to expect from each year, month and day. With your life path clearly mapped out, it will be easy for you to pinpoint the best times to start a new job, focus on family, launch a business, take time to reflect, make a major purchase, complete a project, expand your horizons and more.

"I've used numerology for nearly 30 years. This tool is accurate, exciting, and helpful. *The Power of Time* will show you how."
—Christiane Northrup, MD, author of *Women's Bodies, Women's Wisdom* and *The Wisdom of Menopause*

"A top-notch reference, one that will excite and instruct anyone about the power of numbers in your life."
—*Dell Horoscope*

"This immensely readable book is a fascinating introduction to the subject of numerology. Best of all, *The Power of Time* takes the reader by the hand and shows her how to apply the concepts to her own life. I found the workbook sections especially helpful and could not put the book down until I had charted my own Life Path Number, Personal Year Number and 9-Year Epicycle. *The Power of Time* is a unique and insightful contribution to the many books available on setting goals and making short- and long-term career plans."
—CJ Carmichael, best-selling romance author

www.ingramcontent.com/pod-product-compliance
Lightning Source LLC
Chambersburg PA
CBHW050552300426
44112CB00013B/1877